MW00623593

"A valuable work that will help you think at your best so you create your highest life."

~ Robin Sharma,
#1 worldwide bestselling author of
The Wealth Money Can't Buy

"Above Average is a must-read for anyone looking to unlock their full potential. This book offers a clear, practical guide to harnessing the incredible power of consistent positive thinking. It empowers readers to break free from limiting beliefs, reframe challenges, and cultivate a positive, success-driven mindset. If you're ready to transform your life, this book is an invaluable resource to get you started on the path to success."

~ Joseph William Foster,
founder of Reebok

"Mike's book offers invaluable insights into developing a success mindset. Blending wisdom and understanding with practical techniques, he guides the reader to their own path towards their goals. The book is full of 'a-ha!' moments that will have you reaching for your notebook to make sure that you don't forget them. Read it… and your future self will thank you."

~ Annabelle Beckwith Consultancy |
Coaching | Training | Leadership | Entrepreneurship |
Business scale

"Reading 'Above Average' has been transformative for me. This book is not just a guide but a powerful tool that has inspired me to elevate every aspect of my life. The practical methods Mike Radoor shares are now a part of my daily routine, helping me to constantly reprogram my subconscious mind towards success and fulfillment. The insights into understanding and controlling my subconscious powers have been eye-opening, allowing me to break free from limiting beliefs and tap into my true potential. This book doesn't just motivate; it provides a concrete roadmap for achieving personal growth and living an extraordinary life. 'Above Average' has become a resource that I return to again and again as I work on becoming the best version of myself. It's not just about reading this book; it's about living it, and I'm grateful for the impact it has had on my journey of self-discovery and achievement."

~ David Sandström
David Sandstrøm, Marketing Director of KLARNA

Mike Radoor has written an outstanding book that's easy to follow and full of practical tools to help you become the best version of yourself.

Whether you're just starting out or already experienced, this book offers valuable insights and reminders to elevate your game.

I highly recommend it to anyone looking to succeed and take their life to the next level.

~ Jannik Olander
CEO & Head of Design of NIALAYA JEWELRY

"Mike's book has completely transformed the way I approach my daily mindset and personal goals. It's not just my professional life that's improving—it's also had a profound impact on my private and everyday routines. With better habits and a more positive, focused outlook, I'm seeing real change. This book is an absolute game-changer!"

~ John Arne Riise
Former Professional soccer player, Liverpool

Above Average is a powerful guide to transforming your mindset. The blend of philosophical wisdom and personal experience provides a unique and motivating perspective. I found the strategies easy to follow and incredibly impactful. This book will stay with you long after you finish reading.

~ Judy O'Beirn,
President and CEO of Hasmark Publishing International.

ABOVE
AVERAGE

THE SCIENCE OF
ACHIEVEMENT

MIKE RADOOR

DEDICATION

To my daughter, who I want to grow up with a pure heart, strong mind and a unwavering lust to live life to the fullest.

TABLE OF CONTENTS

INTRODUCTION

Like a witness sworn to testify in court, the pages that follow will give you the truth and nothing but the truth. You're holding a book that **will** transform your life, if you are willing to work for it. You must commit to doing the things this book instructs. You must commit to doing what I tell you to do. You must read it repeatedly to ensure it penetrates your subconscious. But I promise you, once it does, it will take you where you want to go…for the rest of your life.

There is a real reason why some people achieve what they want and others don't. There are clear patterns and strategies that Above Average people demonstrate, which Average and Below Average people do not. Being Above Average isn't difficult; it's a way of thinking and feeling. It's a way of interpreting situations that Average and Below Average people don't utilize. This is not "your fault." It's just something you didn't know. But it is something everyone can learn. This is something YOU will be taught. Not intellectually, per se, but emotionally and subconsciously.

No person is born into an Above Average mindset. No person is born into an Average mindset. We are all born with a neutral mind, ready to learn. We are like a clean sheet of paper, where our story begins when we are presented with the first ideas from whomever is there to present them to us—mainly our parents. The Above Average mind is learned, which is exactly why I'm writing this book. I'm giving you the keys to the kingdom of joy, victory, unlimited love, unlimited power, and 100% control over your life in all possible areas. You must do only three things to embed the Above Average program into your subconscious mind:

1. Study the information in this book.
2. Implement the Above Average Methods week by week.
3. Teach the Method to everyone you meet who wants a successful and fulfilling life.

Only when we study, implement, and teach will this program become fully activated. I will explain to you in detail how it works, while keeping it short and simple. Too many books are written with too much information for the Average mind to comprehend. This book is not one of them. And let's not forget that reading is only part of it. You will need to experience the Method, not just read about it. You will need to feel it, not just understand the words. You will need to study and reread the chapters repeatedly until your subconscious mind accepts the new program. Like much else in life, when you put the work in, you reap the rewards.

This is not philosophy; this is science. Getting results in life is science. Living a meaningful and fulfilled life is an art. Results have protocols. Fulfillment and happiness have individual designs from person to person. If you want to lose weight, there is a scientific formula to follow that applies to all human beings.

If you want to feel fulfilled and happy, and full of joy, drive, and passion, there is individual internal thinking and decision-making that needs to take place.

I will teach you the methods and show you the way to become Above Average. How you use the methods in your life is entirely up to you. With these methods, you will be able to create whatever results you want in any aspect of your life. If you want to be rich, the methods will work. If you want to be famous, the methods will work. If you want to be successful, the methods will work. If you want a deeper and more loving relationship, the methods will work. If you want to live the life of your dreams, the methods will work. If you want to become the best version of yourself, the methods will work. The Above Average Methods are designed to create the results you want in your life.

In writing this book, I didn't hesitate to be concrete and assertive. I've learned from experience that harsh truths are what make people grow. And I want you to grow. I want you to grow fast, steadily, and absolutely. But this book is not about what I want. It is about what you want. So, let me ask you a sincere question, and I want you to be completely honest with yourself: On a scale from 1 to 10, where 1 is absolute zero growth and 10 is maverick growth, how much do you want to grow as a person—financially, mentally, relationship-wise, physically, and spiritually? Take your time to think about this before you read further. Your answer will determine your true growth. In any growth, a breakthrough must happen. Pain is inevitable, but suffering is a choice. Decide right here, right now, that this is your time to grow. This is your time to get what you want in life. This is the time to conquer the Average and expand into the Above Average.

You have all the resources in the world around you. You have all the information available at your fingertips. All you need to do now is decide. For anything to happen in your life, you must act, but before you can truly act, you must decide. Decision is the godfather of action, and action leads to results. This is science. This is what makes or breaks you: your decisions.

It's not about what you achieve that makes you happy. It's about who you grow into as a person that fills your life with meaning and joy. You must aim to make decisions in your life. Remember, decisions ultimately shape your destiny. The food you choose to eat for dinner shapes your body. The person you decide to marry becomes your life. The people you choose to spend time with shape your beliefs, attitudes, values, and life. The career you choose becomes your life. "Decision equals destiny" (Tony Robbins). You must decide to face what's in front of you. You must decide to raise the standards of what you expect from yourself. No matter how magical or less than great your life is at this moment, it's time to grow. It's time to move up to the next level. It's time to go Above Average.

This book is not just about changing how you think but about reprogramming your subconscious mind to align with aspirations of success, fulfillment, and joy beyond the Average. This book will give you concrete methods to do so, to help you become the best version of yourself. This book will teach you how to reach your goals, and how to get rid of negative thoughts. This book will give you the recipe to get whatever you want in your life.

Only an Average mind with a bachelor's degree or higher will ask for evidence, references, and educational background to discuss the legitimacy of things before actually implementing the methods. This book is not written to bore the reader with references of proof. You will find them at the end of the book, not throughout the pages. This book is written to instruct and develop you. It is for those of you who sincerely want to rise Above Average. You shall study the information in this book, implement the Above Average Method week by week, and then teach the Method to everyone you come into contact with who wants a successful and fulfilling life. Only then will these methods work. They won't work if the rubber doesn't meet the road.

The information you hold in your hands will guide you as you strive to achieve your ultimate goals in life. It will provide you with the truths of how an Above Average mind is designed. It will inform, teach, and stimulate you into taking massive action. At the end of the book, you will get a 20-step guide on how to implement the information into your mind and life. This book is written for those who want more in life, whatever that might be. This book is written for those who want more happiness, more joy, and more long-lasting results.

Let's get started so your Above Average life can begin.

PART I

YOUR SUBCONSCIOUS POWERS

Part I will guide you through the fundamental principles of the subconscious mind, revealing how it shapes your reality and how you can master it to adopt an Above Average mind and achieve your goals. You will learn to tap into this boundless source of power and reprogram it with the same certainty and purpose that nature uses to program a seed to become a tree. The journey ahead is one of discovery, transformation, and ultimate achievement as you learn to harness the full potential of your subconscious powers. Keep reading.

CHAPTER 1

UNDERSTANDING YOUR SUBCONSCIOUS POWERS

"Until you make the unconscious conscious, it will direct your life and you will call it fate."

\- Carl Jung

To truly understand the essence of success, you must look to the most flawless example we have: nature itself. Nature operates with absolute success, governed by instincts and cycles that ensure survival, growth, and reproduction. Every element, from the smallest seed to the mightiest predator, follows an inherent script written by millions of years of evolution—an intelligence that science has yet to fully comprehend.

Consider the journey of a plant. It begins as a seed, encapsulating potential within its shell. When given the right conditions—soil, water, and sunlight—it sprouts, breaking through the earth's surface. From there, it grows ceaselessly toward its maximum potential until it can grow no more. This relentless pursuit of growth, driven by an internal blueprint, is nature's way of showcasing success. The plant does not doubt its path; it simply grows, maximizing its potential within its environment. It is not bigger than its environment, but it is a master within it.

The same principle applies to a squirrel. A squirrel gathers as many nuts as it can, without pausing to question its actions. It collects, stores, and prepares, ensuring its survival and the continuation of its species. This tireless effort is a testament to the squirrel's subconscious programming that drives success in nature.

Or take the lion, yet another perfect example of nature's successful recipe. A lion has a natural drive for reproduction and survival. Its life revolves around protecting its territory, ensuring the well-being of its pride, and perpetuating its lineage. The lion does not contemplate its existence or its role; it simply acts. It is driven by instincts that have ensured the survival of its species for generations. This is success!

I could continue with hundreds more examples to prove that the truth of success is born with and by nature. Like the plant, the squirrel, and the lion, we also possess a subconscious mind, a powerful force that governs our actions, beliefs, and ultimately, our success. But unlike other creatures, we humans have the capacity to question, to doubt, and to override our instincts with logic and fear.

Unlike other species found in the natural world, we have unlimited potential. We are equipped with both a conscious and a subconscious mind. We have the ability to think and control our actions and reactions, thoughts, beliefs, habits, decisions, and emotional states. We can grow bigger than our environment. In order to do so, we must first understand how our conscious desires align with our subconscious programming. By removing the barriers to our success, we can grow, collect, and bring our wildest dreams into reality. This is not philosophy; this is fact. Just look around you at what some exceptional humans have accomplished in a single lifetime.

Consider Elon Musk, who revolutionized multiple industries, from electric cars with Tesla to space travel with SpaceX. Think about Jeff Bezos, who transformed the retail world with Amazon. There's also Mark Zuckerberg, who connected billions through Facebook. Don't forget Satya Nadella, who led Microsoft to new heights with cloud computing and AI innovations. Then there's Sundar Pichai, steering Google and Alphabet into the future of technology. And let's not overlook the remarkable journeys of Conor McGregor and Cristiano Ronaldo in the world of sports. McGregor, starting with nothing, became a global icon in mixed martial arts, changing the game with his charisma and fighting skill. Ronaldo worked tirelessly from a young age, overcoming countless challenges to become one of soccer's greatest players, embodying dedication, talent, and relentless ambition.

You're Programmed to Think and Act

Have you ever wondered why you're not getting the results you're looking for in your life? Or why some other person with fewer resources suddenly thrives with full-blown success while you're still sitting on your couch, pointing fingers at who's to blame for your failures? This describes most people. They envy those who make it and label them as "lucky," born with special abilities, or born into wealth, along with thousands of other illusory reasons.

The truth is that resources are available to everyone at any given time. Let's face it, we live in an era where every single resource is accessible at any given time. The biggest illusions we allow in our lives are the reasons we didn't make it. Ask 10 of your friends why they didn't succeed, and they will give you several legitimate reasons, but in fact, they're all illusions. It's never the resources. Rather, it's the lack of resourcefulness. There's a big difference.

Your subconscious mind will always do what you believe to be true. Whatever you believe, you will receive. Your subconscious mind is far more powerful than you can imagine. This is not a lesson they teach in school. Whatever results you have seen in your life up until now are the cause and effect of your paradigms.

Paradigms – Subconscious Programming

From birth until around the age of six, your mind operates in a near-hypnotic state, absorbing and adopting the beliefs, attitudes, and mindsets of those around you—primarily your parents. These beliefs have been passed down through generations, creating a cycle that continues until you decide to challenge and change it. Your subconscious programming (paradigms and belief systems) constructed the foundation of what you believe as truth, which in turn influences every decision you make and every action you take—for the rest of your life. Whatever you feel inside of you becomes your truth. If you feel you are lacking something in life, you will lack it. If you feel you have something in your life, you will get it. It is that simple, yet still very hard for the Average mind to comprehend. This is something I will teach you.

You must learn to understand that it is your subconscious programming that can hold you back from achieving the success you desire. It is what you believe as the truth that empowers or disempowers you. It's not about the hand you were dealt, but rather, how you play your cards. The attitudes and beliefs "installed" in you during your formative years can either fuel your rise to Above Average or anchor you in a sea of mediocrity. And there is nothing wrong with that unless you want to achieve extraordinary things—unless you want to adopt an Above Average mind. Unless you want to reach your ultimate goal in life. Unless you want to become the best version of yourself.

Mark my words when I say that most people will warn you against adopting this attitude. They might tell you that this will cause you stress, disappointment, and failure. Do not listen to them. Stress is how we perceive things, and is mostly caused by worry and fear. It is simply a reaction to your thoughts. You cannot become stressed, depressed, or fail if you have an optimistic, healthy, and positive mind. You cannot fail if you see opportunities all around you. You cannot lack something in your life that you believe is already yours.

Who you are today is the result of your most dominant thoughts, and these thoughts have been programmed into your subconscious mind since childhood. You have also attracted other people with the same belief systems, and here you are: Average or Below Average. It's important to mention that there is nothing wrong with being Average; it is simply a mathematical approach to all the mindsets in the world. If we take 100 people and look at their minds, the Average will be what the majority possess.

To demonstrate, I'll define through an example the Average mind and how this mind was programmed to be that way. Imagine a person named Alex. Since childhood, Alex was surrounded by a loving family, but one that adhered strictly to conventional beliefs about success and failure. Phrases like "We're not the kind of people who start businesses," "Money doesn't grow on trees," and "Just get a stable job and don't take risks" were common. These statements, repeated over time, weren't meant to harm Alex. In fact, they were meant to protect him.

Note: It usually is never meant to harm anyone; it is simply the beliefs of the parents that create the beliefs in ourselves.

However, these constant reminders, words, and limitations acted like a software program installed in Alex's subconscious mind. Alex was programmed to think and believe that these were true. He was helpless. All a child can do in their early years is to look at those around them and adopt their thoughts, feelings, beliefs, and actions.

As Alex grew, this programming influenced every decision he made. When faced with opportunities for advancement or entrepreneurship, Alex's subconscious mind replayed those early lessons: "Don't take risks," "This isn't for people like us," "We'll never get rich," "We're meant to be hard workers, not entrepreneurs."

This deep-seated programming created a hesitancy that blocked him from taking the necessary steps toward his ultimate goals in life, despite Alex's conscious desire to achieve more. We call it being "unconsciously incompetent."

His inner dialogue would talk him down and away from his true power and potential. But it's just an illusion—a subconscious program. In reality, Alex has two arms, two legs, one mouth, and every other physical attribute as anyone who climbs the ladder and lives the life of their dreams. He possesses the same opportunities, but his limiting beliefs prevent him from recognizing them.

Understand that Alex's way of thinking subconsciously created meaning for what his mind focused on, resulting in a lack of achievements in life. Alex's subconscious program will persist until he likely dies unhappy, with unfulfilled dreams.

My advice: Do not be like Alex!

Most people are unaware of these paradigms and the power of the subconscious mind. If they were, there would be far more successful people in the world. They don't realize that their Average mindset, shaped by their programming, holds them back from reaching their full potential and achieving remarkable success.

But this can be updated. This can change. This will change with the information and the Above Average Method outlined in this book. It is the pathway to transforming an Average mind into an Above Average mind. There is a reason why only a few people in the world are truly wealthy: they possess an Above Average mind.

Life is not just about becoming a successful person. It's about growth. Human beings are happiest when they grow. Contrary to popular belief, success is not just about achieving goals. Rather, success is the pursuit of goals that truly matter to you and progressively working toward them. You are already successful if you have a goal and are actively working toward it.

You must understand that you have the power to reprogram your mind. This is exciting! Think about it. You have the power to reprogram your thoughts, beliefs, emotions, decisions, and actions. Through the methods in this book, you will learn to identify, challenge, and replace your limiting beliefs with empowering ones. Give something an empowering meaning, and it changes everything. Likewise, give something a disempowering meaning, and the game is over. To start, we must first learn to control our emotions.

CHAPTER 2

CONTROLLING
YOUR EMOTIONAL SELF

*"The moment you become aware of the ego in you, it is
strictly speaking no longer the ego, but just an old, conditioned mind-pattern. Ego implies unawareness. Awareness
and ego cannot coexist."*

- Osho

At the core of humanity's most confounding dilemmas—
wars, environmental devastation, and acts of violence—
lies a common denominator: the Ego, our Emotional Self. Your
Ego is characterized by irrational and often unchecked emotional reactions that propel you toward actions that are not only
self-destructive but detrimental to society at large.

Think about it for a moment. Why are we destroying the
earth's finest resources, creating climate changes that will eventually kill millions (if not billions) of people? Why are we killing

innocent people in wars over land we all have the right to live on? Why do we say hurtful things to each other, causing shame and guilt? These reactions, deeply ingrained from childhood, dictate a significant portion of our lives through the automatic, subconscious programming discussed in Chapter 1.

We are all born as irrational beings. Robert Greene reminds us that this is a necessity for evolution, but we live in a different time than we did 300,000 years ago. Our societies and needs have changed. We do not need the Ego as much as we did long ago. We do not need to fight for survival in the same intense manner. By mastering your emotions, you not only enhance your own life but contribute to a more rational, understanding, and peaceful world.

To master your emotional self, you must commit to lifelong self-improvement. You must develop yourself, manage emotional fatigue, and recognize reaction patterns. When you learn to master your Ego (emotional self), you can begin to rewrite the subconscious programs that have long directed your actions and open yourself to the limitless potential of an Above Average life.

Your Ego has an insatiable appetite for recognition and dominance and frequently hijacks your better judgment, leading to impulsive and sometimes catastrophic decisions. It is not rational; it is irrational. You must learn to control your emotional self and understand the triggers of your Ego. That begins with self-awareness.

Self-Awareness

To control your emotional self, you must cultivate self-awareness. Self-awareness involves constant observation and reflection on your thoughts, feelings, and motivations. You must learn to ask yourself why you feel a certain way and whether your immediate reaction serves your long-term interests and values. When you learn to respond rather than react—to choose actions aligned with rational judgment instead of being swept away by emotion—you will experience growth far beyond what you have ever imagined. Your emotional self is your mental prison, keeping you locked up and unable to achieve your ultimate goals.

Self-awareness also requires an understanding of empathy. Learn to see situations from others' perspectives. What does this have to do with being aware of yourself? When you master your emotional self, it becomes easier not to react to other people's irrational actions because you will recognize that others are also driven by their emotional selves. This fosters patience and compassion, essential qualities for navigating social relationships and conflicts. It is through empathy that you can transcend your egoistic tendencies and connect with others on a more profound, meaningful level. Read that last sentence again.

Later in this book, you will find exact methods to reprogram your emotional self. Control it and direct it toward an Above Average mindset. It is the most rational people in the world who harvest the long-term benefits, and the most irrational who damage themselves, the world, and others the most. But first, it's important to remember to take your suggestions seriously.

Take Your Suggestions Seriously

You must take your suggestions seriously. As we discussed in Chapter 1, whatever thoughts you entertain repeatedly will either block or enhance your extraordinary results. The majority of people grow up in mediocrity, bombarded with negativity, limitations, fear, and jealousy since childhood. Phrases like: "You can't," "You're going nowhere," "Don't even try," "You're bound to fail," "Forget it, you don't stand a chance," "You're all wrong," "It's a waste of time," "Everything's going to go bad," "Why bother, no one cares," "Trying hard is pointless," "You're past your prime in life," "Things are only getting worse," "Life's a constant fight," "Love's a joke," "You're doomed to lose," "Bankruptcy is just around the corner," "Beware, the virus is coming for you," "Trust no one," and on and on.

These words have entered your subconscious mind and have become your truth. If that's the case, you must decide to change your suggestions (mental dialogue) and take control with another type of self-talk (suggestions). Your mental dialogue works like an old tape that keeps playing, setting you up for fear, failure, negativity, envy, and depression.

It is well-known in psychology that what we say, think, and feel often becomes our reality. It is also a well-known tool for changing our behaviors. For over a century, hypnotic suggestion has been used to successfully treat a wide range of clinical conditions, including chronic and acute pain, post-traumatic stress disorder, phobias, eating disorders, and others. And this is something the Average mind will never know or hear about. You must understand that what you say to yourself on a daily basis becomes your beliefs, and what you believe becomes your life.

Numerous studies have shown the power that suggestion has on our subconscious minds. Hypnotherapy is one way of proving the effects of suggestions. Even the marketing industry uses suggestions on a multibillion-dollar scale to get you to eat, drink, smoke, or stare at their products or services. There's a reason why Coca-Cola wins—they are the best hypnotizers out there. There is a reason why Corona beer wins—they are the best hypnotizers out there. There is a reason why you do not believe in yourself, why you don't take action, and why you haven't achieved your dreams. You've been hypnotized to believe you can't. It's that simple! Instead, learn to understand and accept this fact before you can change it for the better.

Be Mindful of the News You Read

Every time you read the news, it's like opening a Pandora's box of negativity: failure, fear, worry, anxiety, doom—it's all there. So, if you read the news every day, you're setting yourself up to take on that emotional toll. I am convinced that the majority of journalists are good people, but we must accept that they work for capitalist employers that need to sell. Nothing draws readers to the news more than drama, fear, and chaos. Fear equals revenue. Fearful or dramatic headlines equal readers, which equals revenue. Choose what you read on a daily basis carefully. If you want to read the news, read proactively, not reactively.

Rearrange Social Media

You also need to start rearranging your social media. Be proactive in who you follow and what you like or comment on. The algorithms are designed to show you more of what you engage in. Engage in drama, and you will get more drama. Engage in self-development, positive psychology, mindset mastery, habits, and successful people, and you will get more of that. Every time your eyes read from your screen, it activates a cascade of thoughts. Choose your social media following wisely.

Be Cautious of Other Negativity

Watch out for the negativity coming at you. You don't have to get sucked into whatever comes your way. Be aware and choose to act, not react. We've all been immersed in negativity from our earliest days, growing up, and even as teens. Think about it, and you'll notice a pattern.

Family, friends, teachers, co-workers—they've all contributed to feeding us a steady stream of negative vibes, often disguised as 'advice.' Much of this 'advice' is about shaping you to fit someone else's idea of perfection, making you think and act in ways that benefit them, not you. Understand that most people do not intend to harm you; they just want to advise you from their perspective. However, you must discern if they are mostly negative or positive.

You will find that most people are generally negative. This is a fact. Starting today, be aware whenever you speak with anyone. Identify if what they say is positive or negative. You will find more negativity, and you need to ignore it. Instead, listen to your own positive self-talk that lifts you up. Remember, you control your mind. You can accept or reject any idea that comes your way.

You have this power!

Let me give you an example: Think of a red elephant. Are you thinking of a red elephant? Good! Now think of a black cat. Do you see it? Good! Now think of what you want to think about. You see, you have the power to choose what you think and what you focus on. You must learn to train this skill. You must learn to reject negative thoughts and replace them with positive ones, just as I replaced the red elephant with the black cat for you.

Remove Yourself from Negative Hypnotizers

"You're the average of the five people you spend the most time with."

- Dan Peña

Dan Peña, the "50 Billion Dollar Man," did not come from wealth. He made it big because he knew something unique: how to use the power of positive thinking and the magic of believing you can do something, even when it's tough. And he wasn't alone. Many others knew this too. Let's take a look at some powerful examples:

- Bob Proctor, a legend in motivation, emphasized the power of your thoughts. He taught that all the "secret stuff" happens in your mind. It's about the positive things you tell yourself and how you handle the negativity the world throws at you. He advised feeding your mind with the good stuff and watching how everything changes for the better.

- Tony Robbins, a true powerhouse for positivity, emphasizes the importance of monitoring the thoughts and ideas you let into your mind, ensuring they propel you forward rather than hold you back. Tony teaches you how to control your thoughts and emotional state through focus. You can change your life in a heartbeat.

- Jim Rohn, another giant in the personal development space, taught us to be careful about what we let into our minds. Jim compared the mind to a garden that needs to be tended, ensuring only the good seeds are allowed to grow. He taught us to be the guard of our own mind and that our thoughts will nurture whatever seeds they come from: negativity or positivity.

- Brian Tracy, a big name in motivation and success, also stresses the importance of maintaining positive thoughts. Brian emphasizes setting goals, believing in yourself, and using positive affirmations to align your subconscious with what you want to achieve.

All these guys are saying pretty much the same thing: Your mind is powerful. What you spend your time thinking about is what you will become. This is not new knowledge. This has existed since the days of the Bible, which says: "Whatever is noble, whatever is right, whatever is pure, whatever is lovely, whatever is admirable—if anything is excellent or praiseworthy—think about such things" (Philippians 4:8). Or in Proverbs 23:7: "For as he thinketh in his heart, so is he."

I'm not trying to impress you by using references. What I am trying to do is show you that there is an abundance of information on this very subject. Through my own self-study, which includes reading more than 600 self-development and human psychology books, taking six courses in human psychology, studying mindset, habits, and life coaching, and founding three international multimillion-dollar companies, my conclusion is that you will be influenced by those you spend the most time with. You will start to adopt their suggestions and beliefs. In fact, you will never be more than 5% better than those you spend the most time with.

You've got to listen carefully to what people around you keep repeating. If their words are in any way limiting or negative, reject them and start looking for others to spend time with. Their minds are keeping you hypnotized to be forever Average, and that's not what you want. I know that to be true because you're reading this book, so pay attention to their repeating suggestions. I guarantee you they are not even aware of it themselves. They got it from someone else too. We're not born saying these things; we are taught to say them.

Remember, your subconscious mind is very powerful. It will support you in anything your conscious mind decides to accept. When you start doubting yourself or focusing on what you think are your weak spots—saying things like "I can't do this," "I'm too old for that," or "I don't have the right background"—you're setting yourself up for failure. It's like putting roadblocks in your own way, making life harder than it needs to be. Whatever your conscious mind accepts, your subconscious mind directs.

When you make excuses or tell yourself you can't do something, you won't do it. You have unlimited potential and strength inside you, but negative thinking will lead to feeling down, scared, and blocked. Remember: Whatever you feel will be your truth. Learn to change this. You must start to believe in yourself by thinking and talking in positive terms. The Above Average Method will teach you the exact steps to do so.

Think about it. What gives you the most self-confidence and belief in yourself? Saying things like, "I am too dumb," "I can't do this," "I am too old," "I am nothing compared to…" Or, is it by saying things like, "I can do whatever I want," "I am made for greatness," "I am smart, fast, and self-confident"? The answer is obvious.

Learn to say the right things to yourself. Ask yourself the right questions and give yourself pep talks to get moving. You already have the power; you just don't believe it yet. You must believe it before you can achieve it. I'm sure you've heard this before. You might have read it in *The Secret* by Rhonda Byrne, *Think and Grow Rich* by Napoleon Hill, *The Power of Positive Thinking* by Norman Vincent Peale, *The Alchemist* by Paulo Coelho, *The Power of Now* by Eckhart Tolle, or even in the Bible: Matthew 21:22 (NIV): "If you believe, you will receive whatever you ask for in prayer."

Your subconscious mind acts on what your conscious mind accepts as the truth. Therefore, you must keep your thoughts positive and hang out with people who lift you up. Think about it. LeBron James did not make it big by hanging around people who didn't believe in him or had nothing positive to say. You have to surround yourself with positivity, aim high, and cultivate positive self-talk. It starts with your thoughts. It starts with your self-talk. Your self-talk turns into your beliefs, and what you believe you can achieve, you will achieve.

Maybe this information is new to you, maybe it is not. Whatever the case, remember, knowing it is not the same as doing it. Up until now, you might have known it, but you didn't do it. You must start to act on this knowledge. Maybe you were never aware of how your friends approach their lives. Maybe you have been thinking, "My friends aren't negative…" My bet is that the majority of them are. Very few people in the world are genuinely positive. Very few. Start to become aware of this and either reject their suggestions or remove yourself from their influence.

An Exercise in Positivity

Start repeating these affirmations to yourself a minimum of 50 times a day to counteract the negative hypnosis you've experienced throughout your life. Begin this practice right now and see how magically it works. Remember—this is not philosophy; this is science.

- "I can achieve anything I set my mind to."
- "I am destined for greatness."
- "I am free to make my own choices."
- "I am built for success."

- "I seize every opportunity that comes my way."
- "I am on the right path."
- "My efforts are always worth it."
- "My knowledge and skills open doors."
- "I am making positive changes in the world."
- "My actions are valued and make a difference."
- "Hard work leads me to amazing places."
- "I am always learning and growing."
- "There's no limit to what I can accomplish."
- "Every day brings me closer to my goals."
- "Life is full of opportunities for success."
- "Love enriches my life in beautiful ways."
- "I am a winner."
- "My financial future is secure."
- "I am protected, and I will stay healthy."
- "I trust in the goodness of people."
- "It's never too late for me to succeed."
- "I am resilient against life's challenges."
- "Every day is a chance to become better."
- "I am surrounded by love and support."
- "I am a powerful creator of my own life story."

You must make this practice a part of your everyday routine, and do so for the rest of your life. In the later chapters in this book, I will teach you how to do this. But for now, how do you know what it is that you really want? Keep reading to find out.

CHAPTER 3

YOU MUST FOCUS ON WHAT YOU WANT AND WHY YOU WANT IT

"People with goals succeed because they know where they're going."

- Earl Nightingale

Think of your subconscious mind as a GPS, guiding you to your desires with laser precision. Your mind is equipped with a smart system called the Reticular Activating System (RAS). This system becomes active when you focus on something specific. For example, when you wanted a red car, you suddenly started seeing red cars everywhere. If you wanted a fit body, you began noticing fit people everywhere. Or perhaps you wanted a loving life partner, and you started seeing couples showing intimacy all around you.

Do you recognize this? Whatever you focus on subconsciously, you will start seeing everywhere. You begin getting ideas to achieve what you want but also what you do not want. If you focus on what you do not want, you will see how impossible it is to get rid of it.

You must learn to focus on what you want, not on what you do not want. If you always worry about what could go wrong, you will start seeing all the risks. If you focus on what you want, you will start seeing all the opportunities. If most of your thoughts are: "No way, not happening," your RAS will ensure that's your reality, pointing out every reason something won't work out.

You must focus on what you really want—what you truly want—and keep that goal in your mind at all times. Remember that wherever focus goes, energy flows. You might have heard that before too, so start accepting this information and act on it.

Average and Below Average minds often stay trapped in a state of hypnosis regarding their own capabilities and what they can achieve. You must understand that this is just a mental drama. It is not real. It only becomes real when you believe it as the truth. This is why so many people remain in an Average mind, preventing them from living the life they truly desire. Through my experience working with thousands of people who want more out of life, I've encountered many who, when asked about their goals, never thought about it. Most of them, however, often thought about what they did not want.

Traps You Can Get Caught In

There are many mental traps that can ensnare you when you want something so badly that you're constantly thinking of it.

You need to understand that it is your feeling of already having it that makes the "magic" happen. Cristiano Ronaldo knew he would be the greatest long before he became it. Conor McGregor knew he would be the greatest long before he became it.

The majority of people get stuck on how to do it, and this scares them from taking massive action. This is a mental trap. This is what Below Average and Average minds do. You must overcome this to gain the Above Average mentality. You must understand that anything is possible, and you do not have to know everything about how to do it. The answers will come to you from your subconscious mind as long as you instruct it directly with what you want. Be precise and make sure you do not want too many things at the same time. Find a top-level goal that, when reached, will allow you to acquire the rest.

Knowing What You Want

I recently had a conversation with a middle-aged mother on Instagram. She responded to a story where I emphasized the importance of setting goals. She asked, "What if you don't know what you want? I have so many interests and am curious about many things, but at 37, I still don't quite know what I want career-wise."

I responded directly, pointing out that she likely did know what she wanted but had never taken the time to deeply consider it. I reminded her, "Life isn't just about your career. It's much more. Imagine you have a magic wand and can have EVERYTHING you want EXACTLY as you wish 5-10 years from now. Where do you live? How do you live? What's your income? How much do you work? What does your family look like? What are you driving?"

Her reply was typical of the Average mind, focusing solely on her career as dictated by societal norms, showing the deep-rooted influence of capitalism. The capitalistic system has conditioned us to think about what we can become within the system rather than what we truly want in life. This is a programmed way of thinking. Reflect on this for a moment. Do you know what job title you want more than the life you want to live?

Continuing the conversation, she acknowledged, "It's definitely more than that. But I still think that for many, their hobbies and interests have also become their lifestyle or career. Those are good questions, and I find them difficult to answer, especially considering I also have three children to think about. But I will try to write it down. I've never had a family to guide me. I've been on my own since the age of 17, and twenty years later, with three teenagers, I still don't quite know where I want to be in life. I've faced many demons and have come to forgive and accept a lot! So, I'm in a good place. But I'm treading water trying to figure out which harbor I want to explore. I've been to quite a few places without finding peace, or perhaps the belief in allowing myself the tranquility and pride in what I've achieved."

You may find yourself in a similar trap. Think of the following:

- What do you really want? Not what career do you want, but what lifestyle do you want and what life do you want to live?

- What do you really love to do?

- What are you good at—or even better, what would you *like* to become good at?

- How much money do you want to earn?

- How much money do you want to possess?

- And most importantly, why do you want it? Why do you want to live a life like that? Why do you want to make that amount of money?

When you know what you want and why you want it, your RAS will attract how to get it for you. It's never about the "how." It is always about the "what" and the "why." You will learn how to get what you want, but not what and why you want it. This has to come from deep inside of you. The rest you will learn.

Affirmations

When you think of what you want but still feel you do not have it, you are trapped in the feeling of lacking it. Let me explain. Let's say you want 1 million dollars in your account. You want it so badly that you think about it all the time. However, when you look at your bank account and see only $2,000, you subconsciously tell yourself, "It will never come. Who am I to think I can get $1,000,000?!" This mental trap will not serve you. It may be hard to understand now, but let me explain further.

Becoming wealthy (or achieving anything else) starts with a deep-seated belief that you're already there. Most people who believe in affirmations are not doing it right. When they try to manifest their desires, they end up in mental conflicts between what they consciously want and what their subconscious actually believes. Repeating to yourself, "I am a millionaire. I am a millionaire," won't work if you don't truly believe it. Your subconscious mind will recognize the lie, confirm that you are not, and you will attract exactly that: not becoming a millionaire.

The majority of people lack the unseen (mental) resources to support their dreams. They want something in their life but do not believe they can or will ever get it. You must understand that this is just a belief, but it is a belief rooted in your subconscious program. You will need the right mental techniques to actually believe it. Take me, for example. I firmly believe I am always wealthy. Deep down, I know I can create whatever I desire. That belief makes me wealthy and provides me with creative ideas. A person stuck in an "I'm broke" mindset only sees obstacles and finds themselves in situations filled with scarcity. In contrast, someone bursting with ideas to generate wealth finds themselves surrounded by everything they need: ideas and zero fear, just absolute trust. As the Bible says in Matthew 21:22: "And whatever things you ask in prayer, really believing, you will receive." When you are absolutely sure about it, things will manifest. This is also what the Law of Attraction teaches. You can only attract what you truly believe.

Try the following exercise and use it in your daily life as much as possible:

You might be thinking, "I need wealth and success," and that's great. But you must understand that you already have wealth and success if you just believe it. So, it's better to affirm to yourself multiple times a day: "Wealth," "Success." These words represent the "inner power" of your subconscious mind. Don't say, "I am wealthy," because your subconscious mind will catch a lie in an instant (mental conflict). But with words like "Wealth" or "Success" alone, there's no conflict. When you repeat these words often enough, the corresponding feeling emerges, and that's what we're after. The feeling of wealth creates wealth. The feeling of success breeds success. Keep telling yourself these words all the time. Your subconscious acts like a bank of feelings and will manifest whatever you deposit frequently enough.

When I started Miinto.com, I caught the feeling of success. I felt like a millionaire before it became a reality. That certainty came from knowing, without a doubt, it would happen because I was working with two major entrepreneurs who founded the gigantic food delivery platform JustEat. That was my path back then. I've worked with many who told me they were repeating, "I'm a millionaire" or "I'm successful," but deep down, they felt like they were lying to themselves. This is the trap. Your affirmations need to be specific and must not create a mental conflict. That's why it's best to use words that don't cause conflict. Words like "Health," "Harmony," "Happiness," "Wealth," "Success," etc.

You must avoid making negative deposits into the "bank" (subconscious mind) with phrases such as "I don't have enough to make ends meet," "I lack XYZ," or "I'm losing my house because of high interest rates." When you feel fear about the future, that's when you attract more of it into your life. Your subconscious takes those negative feelings (feelings = you believe it) and feeds you obstacles, delays, scarcity, and limitations.

Those who feel wealthy attract more wealth. Those who feel they are lacking attract more lack. The Above Average Method will teach you this later on in the book. Keep reading.

Knowing the Difference Between What You Want Now and What You Want Most

Average and Below Average minds are often reactive. They tend to do what feels good rather than what is right. They tend to do what they want now rather than what they want most. They tend to procrastinate rather than take action. And that is exactly what keeps them from achieving their goals—the fear of "pain" or, even worse, the allure of pleasure. Understand the difference between what you want now versus what you want the most.

Most people fall into the trap of instant gratification—grabbing that extra slice of pizza, binge-watching TV shows, or endlessly scrolling through social media. While these activities may provide immediate pleasure, they distract you from your real goals. Why does this happen? It happens because big corporations have mastered the art of exploiting our desire for comfort and pleasure, profiting immensely from our habits.

Think about this. In the 1950s, life made you move. People walked more, engaged in physical labor, and were generally healthier and happier. Fast forward to the 2020s, and everything is conveniently accessible. Food, entertainment, shopping—you name it. This convenience has led to laziness, weight gain, and, paradoxically, increased unhappiness. It's a counterproductive cycle, and most people don't even realize it. This is the essence of a capitalistic trap. As consumption increases, happiness decreases, leading to even more consumption. Another trap!

These companies, the ones making everything so easy for us, are getting filthy rich because they've tapped into our basic instinct: we all want to feel good with as little effort as possible. When you chase easy pleasures all the time, you are holding yourself back from achieving what you truly want in life. Let me prove it to you. Studies comparing life in the 1950s to today show a significant increase in depression and obesity. Why? Because as life got more comfortable, we started moving less, doing less, and, let's be honest, achieving less. Learn to understand this to rise to an Above Average mind.

Think about the following:

- You want a fit, healthy, and strong body, but yet, you avoid the gym, and eat pizza, cake, and candy.
- You want financial freedom, but you keep giving minimum effort to break out of the Average performance.
- You want a deep connection with your life partner, but you never structure up your relationship conversations, goals, and therapy sessions.
- You want a life full of adventure, but you keep scrolling social media and binge-watching Netflix multiple hours a day.

Our biggest survival instinct is now damaging our physical, mental, and spiritual health, and it is all part of a program deep inside you. Your subconscious mind has accepted this way of living for you. It behaves like a Chief Operating Officer under the CEO—your conscious mind. However, your conscious mind is weakened by the comforts the world constantly pushes you to believe are "The Best for You." Read that again.

Large corporations have found a way to hypnotize you with commercials showing love, peace, and happiness while drinking their products. Your conscious mind accepts this idea, and your subconscious mind reinforces these beliefs. For instance, even one or two sugary drinks a day could increase your risk of Type 2 diabetes by more than 20%. Sugar intake is linked to high blood pressure, high cholesterol, and excess fat, all of which increase the risk of heart disease.

Sugary drinks have also been linked to an increased risk of pancreatic cancer. So why do we consume them on such a large scale? Because we've been misled and hypnotized! If I ask 1,000 people if they want high blood pressure, high cholesterol, excess fat, cancer, and depression, all 1,000 would say, "No, of course not!" But they keep drinking these beverages. Why? Because they're hypnotized and their minds are Average or below. It may be a harsh truth to accept, but it's the truth nonetheless.

You must know the difference between what you want now and what you want most. You don't want cancer, but you crave sugary drinks. You don't want to be overweight, but you consume excess calories. You don't want a job you hate, but you desire an easy way out. You don't want a broken relationship, but you prioritize your immediate desires over lasting connection and understanding. You must understand that your craving for instant gratification is leading you away from your deeper, long-term goals. The Above Average Method sets you free from this matrix. It teaches you to choose what you want most over what you want now, and remember, your subconscious mind has the power to heal. Keep reading.

CHAPTER 4

YOUR SUBCONSCIOUS MIND HAS THE POWER TO HEAL

"The mind and body are not separate units, but one inte-grated system. How we act and what we think, eat, and feel are all related to our health."

- Brian Weiss

As you've seen from the previous chapters, your subcon-scious mind is a powerful part of you. It has the power to heal you from almost everything. But here's the catch—it can heal, but it can also destroy. It is your subconscious mind that promotes anxiety, stress, physical and emotional pain, mood disorders, phobias, and good or bad habits. It controls your self-image, and your self-image controls your actions. And your actions control your destiny.

Your subconscious mind controls your life, but you have the ability to instruct it with the life you want to live. The feelings you want to feel. The actions you want to take. As discussed earlier, your conscious mind is the CEO and your subconscious mind is your COO. Your CEO (the conscious mind) instructs the COO (the subconscious mind) on what to believe by accepting ideas. Once an idea is accepted by the conscious mind, the subconscious mind has no choice but to act upon it. It can only accept what your conscious mind has accepted.

Consider this for a moment. Your subconscious mind controls every living organ in your body. It controls your 40 billion cells each second. It manages your heartbeat, breathing, and the 86 billion neurons in your brain. Your mind is an electrochemical mega-machine. Your 86 billion neurons are each firing off 5-50 messages (action potentials) per second. This activity allows you to process your environment, move your muscles, and maintain balance! All are controlled by your COO (subconscious mind) and led by your CEO (conscious mind). Do not get overwhelmed by these numbers and do not take them for granted, which most people do. They simply don't know.

Let me give you an example. You cut your finger one morning while slicing a beautiful, warm, oven-baked bread. Your conscious mind immediately registers the pain, triggering the 86 billion neurons in your brain to fire off 5-50 messages per second, alerting you to the danger. You drop the knife and reach for the emergency kit. Meanwhile, your subconscious mind, in a matter of milliseconds, has already begun the healing process. Before you even drop the knife, your subconscious mind has instructed your body to start a complex cascade of biological responses aimed at healing the cut. Platelets in your blood clump together at the site of the injury to form a clot, stopping the bleeding. White blood cells rush to the scene to fight off any potential infection, while growth factors are released to promote tissue healing. This entire process, orchestrated by your subconscious mind, showcases the body's incredible ability to heal itself quickly and precisely.

In the days following the cut, the healing process continues without your conscious awareness. New cells grow to replace the damaged ones, and the skin gradually repairs itself, often leaving little trace of the original injury. This incredible journey from injury to recovery highlights the remarkable capabilities of your subconscious mind. Silently and efficiently, it guides the efforts of your 86 billion neurons, tirelessly working to keep you healthy and whole.

A Healing Mindset

But what is our subconscious mind actually capable of healing? Can it heal cancer? Can it cure deadly diseases? Can it resolve mental disorders? The answer is still unknown, but why some people suddenly get healed out of nothing but complete faith remains a mystery science can't fully explain yet either. Understand that there is much information science hasn't been able to prove yet, and just because science can't prove it, it does not mean it isn't happening. One example is the placebo effect—a well-documented phenomenon where healing occurs due to the belief in the efficacy of a treatment rather than the treatment itself. This serves as a clear testament to the mind's power over the body.

I stand among a lineage of thinkers, authors, and philosophers who have long championed the incredible power of the healing mindset. This isn't a novel concept that sprung from Average minds but a truth recognized and revered throughout millennia. To illustrate this timeless principle, let's reflect on a profound passage from the Bible: "Jesus said unto him, if thou canst believe, all things are possible to him that believeth" (Mark 9:23). This scripture captures the essence of faith's transformative power. I advocate for a holistic approach to health that encompasses the physical, mental, and spiritual dimensions of well-being.

Whatever you firmly believe, you shall indeed receive. This belief isn't just a hope or a wish; it's a deep, unshakable confidence in the outcome. Complete faith. You must understand that this faith must happen with ease. Just believe, and it will happen. Believing in this is far beyond what the Average or Below Average mind will do. You must start believing. You must start to have faith. You must start to practice faith. You must learn to have complete faith in your subconscious mind for it to do its work. You must surround yourself completely with faith in everything you want in your life. Understand that having faith is a choice. You must choose it. Conversely, I believe we live much better lives believing in healing rather than disease. This is important. Let me make it very clear that I was never raised in religious beliefs. I wasn't raised in church or any religion, but I started my own spiritual journey, healing my mind and body with nothing but complete faith. Nothing else.

Ancient Wisdom

Throughout history, cultures worldwide have grasped the powerful connection between the mind, body, and spirit, recognizing the profound impact faith and the subconscious mind have on healing. This isn't a modern concept; ancient civilizations deeply understood the relationship between conscious belief and the subconscious mind's ability to influence health and well-being. Here are three ancient practices that demonstrate this timeless wisdom:

Ancient Egyptian Healing: The ancient Egyptians believed in the unity of body and mind, using rituals, temple sleep, and various hypnotic states to stimulate the body's healing processes. Their medical practices included purification and the use of touch, alongside strong faith in the healing process, emphasizing the mind's crucial role in recovery. Both Greeks and Egyptians saw health as a balance, integrating physical and spiritual well-being with treatments that combined prayers, incantations, and remedies revealed by the gods in dreams.

Maya Healing Practices: For the ancient Maya, health was about achieving balance, viewing humans as an integral part of the cosmos. They adopted a holistic approach, focusing on both spiritual and physical well-being to treat imbalances. Maya healers worked to balance the flow of life force within the body, similar to *qi* in traditional Chinese medicine. They used cacao as a medicinal remedy for its health benefits and conducted sweat baths for purification.

Native American Healing: Native American medicine emphasizes the sacred connection between humans and nature, using herbal remedies passed down through generations to promote wellness. They believed in cleansing the body and spirit with sage, seeking peace and spiritual healing through tobacco,

and using cedar for its purifying and healing prop-
erties. Their holistic approach connected the mind,
body, and spirit, underscoring the importance of
environmental health for individual well-being.

These ancient practices reveal a profound understanding of
the healing power of faith and the subconscious mind. These
principles align with modern teachings that emphasize positive thinking, goal setting, and maintaining a health-oriented
mindset. Throughout history, belief has been the ultimate
game-changer.

Consider Matthew 17:20: "He replied, 'Because you have so
little faith. Truly I tell you, if you have faith as small as a mustard
seed, you can say to this mountain, 'Move from here to there,'
and it will move. Nothing will be impossible for you.'"

The Average or Below Average mind might dismiss these
ideas as nonsense until they experience the power of hypnotherapy principles for themselves. Skeptics will remain until
they open up to belief. Our subconscious mind taps into what
I call the infinite mind, where all creation happens. It can heal,
generate abundance, and bring happiness faster than any other
method. Keep reading to discover how.

You Must Lead Your Subconscious Mind Toward What You Want

It's hard for the Average and Below Average mind to grasp what
I am about to share, but bear with me and read this multiple times if needed. Dr. Joe Dispenza, a visionary on a mission
beyond the ordinary, unveiled a staggering truth in the docu-
mentary *What the Bleep Do We Know?* A healthy human mind

processes more than 20 million bits of information every second, yet we're only consciously aware of approximately 40 bits. This discrepancy exists because the conscious mind isn't powerful enough to process all the information that constitutes reality.

Your subconscious mind retains your experiences, concepts, insights, and perceptions long after your conscious mind has forgotten them. These stored elements influence your con- scious self, behaviors, habits, decision-making, and mindset. Yet, you have full control over this process. You possess the power to dictate what your subconscious mind should guide you toward because it is always guiding you—processing 20 million bits versus the 40 bits your conscious mind handles.

You must think positively for your subconscious mind to work positively. You must focus on opportunities to see opportunities. You must think inspirationally to feel inspired. You are a product of your thoughts. Your subconscious mind does not argue with you; it accepts what your conscious mind accepts. If you say, "I cannot afford it," you might be right, but don't express it. Choose a better thought instead, such as, "I will buy it. I accept it in my mind." The Average or Below Average mind might respond with skepticism, but understanding and practicing this concept is crucial.

SOURCE; The Biology of Belief by Dr Bruce Lipton.

You might be thinking, "But that's not true; why should I lie to myself?" I understand your concern, but remember, your subconscious mind does not argue with you or talk back. It accepts what you believe, and what you believe you will see more of.

Wayne Dyer once said, "You see it when you believe it." The Average mind says: "I believe it when I see it." Do you see the difference? The distinction is profound.

You must direct your attention toward what you want at all times. It is only when you focus on what you want that ideas and opportunities will come to you. Your conscious mind is the gatekeeper to your subconscious mind. Its CEO function is to protect your subconscious mind from false impressions. Choose by will to believe that something good will happen and that it is happening now. This is your greatest capacity as a human being.

The Capacity to Choose

Choose happiness, success, and abundance. It might not make sense to you now, but you must do it anyway. I'm not here to delve into the deep psychology and science behind it. My purpose is to guide you toward your wildest dreams. I'm here to provide short, precise, and concrete instructions. This is what I want. This is what I do.

There will be times when you focus on what you want, and things won't progress quickly enough. This is normal. When this happens, remind yourself that you will get what you need when you absolutely need it, not before. Maintain complete faith. Keep believing and instructing your subconscious mind with positive and prosperous thoughts. This is the hardest part, but you have the power to choose your thoughts. Use it! This is what is difficult for the Average and Below Average mind to grasp.

They have been programmed for fear, anxiety, stress, and negativity. Not by choice, but by societal conditioning. This is how we think and feel in larger groups. This is what I call the Average Magnet. The Gravity of Average. Don't get frustrated with my choice of words. I am telling you the truth. I am showing you the way out. I am instructing you on how to go Above Average and beyond, but for that to happen, you must follow my guidance precisely. You must overcome your inner pessimism and fear. Replace words such as "I can't," "I'm not made for success," "I am too poor," "I am not educated enough," "I am too old," "I am too young," or "I will never become what I want to become," with more positive and empowering suggestions.

Let me prove it to you with a simple explanation. Consider two people. One person lives a tremendously successful and fulfilling life. The other person lives a depressed and poor life. If we were to script what they were thinking all day long, you would see the clear difference. If we could print every word, every thought, and every belief, it would be very evident to you.

Person A: Successful and Fulfilling Life

Words:

- "Opportunities are everywhere."
- "Challenges are just opportunities in disguise."
- "I am destined for greatness."
- "I create my own path and walk it with confidence."
- "Success is a result of my actions and mindset."
- "I am a magnet for positive outcomes."
- "I have the power to shape my destiny."
- "Every obstacle I overcome makes me stronger."
- "I am surrounded by abundance and prosperity."
- "I invest in myself and my future."

Thoughts:

- "I'm grateful for every experience that has led me to this moment."

- "I'm excited about what today will bring."
- "My potential is limitless."
- "I trust in my abilities to make the best decisions for myself."
- "Every day is a new chance to create the life I want."
- "My hard work is paying off in ways I can't even imagine."
- "I am always learning and growing."
- "Positivity is a choice I make every moment."
- "I deserve happiness and success."
- "My goals are within reach."

Beliefs:

- "The universe conspires to help me succeed."
- "I am worthy of every good thing that comes my way."
- "I am the architect of my life; the blueprint is my ongoing work."
- "There is a positive side to every situation, and I find it."
- "Believing in myself is a choice that I make daily."
- "I am resilient and can get through any challenge."
- "My happiness is my responsibility."
- "Success is a journey, not a destination."
- "I am capable of achieving whatever I set my mind to."
- "My actions create a ripple effect of positivity in the world."

Person B: Depressed and Poor Life

Words:

- "Why does this always happen to me?"
- "I'll never be as good as others."
- "I'm just not lucky."
- "Nothing I do ever matters."
- "Life is too hard and not worth the effort."
- "I'm just meant to be in the background."
- "It's not like things will get better anyway."
- "I'm always overlooked and undervalued."
- "I don't have what it takes to succeed."
- "Everyone else has it easier than me."

Thoughts:

- "I'm just not meant for happiness."
- "I don't have the energy to try anymore."
- "What's the point when I'll just fail?"
- "No one understands or cares about me."
- "I'm trapped in my circumstances."
- "I'm always one step behind everyone else."
- "It's not fair that others have it so easy."
- "I'm destined to struggle forever."
- "I'm too weak to handle life's challenges."
- "My dreams are just that—dreams, not reality."

Beliefs:

- "Life is fundamentally unfair."
- "People like me don't get to have a happy ending."
- "There's no use in trying to change my fate."
- "I'm not in control of my life."
- "If something can go wrong for me, it will."
- "My past defines my future."
- "I don't deserve success or happiness."
- "The world is against me."
- "I lack what others are born with that leads to success."
- "My beliefs don't matter; nothing ever changes."

My question to you now is: Which one would you prefer to emulate in terms of thinking, speaking, and believing? Which individual do you believe would achieve the best results in life—Person A or Person B? If your answer is Person A, continue reading. If your answer is Person B, discard this book.

Believe Your Goal Is Already Achieved

No successful individual has ever realized their dreams without setting specific, clear, and ambitious goals. This is a universal principle evident in every field of achievement. You must establish and pursue goals—not just any goals, but those that push the boundaries of your imagination and determination. Goals that don't make you a little uneasy are simply not grand enough. They must resonate with your deepest aspirations.

Believing that your goal is already accomplished is a transformative mindset. This concept is not new; it has been the foundation of countless success stories for decades, especially since the rise of the New Thought movement in the early 19th century.

- Take Napoleon Hill's *Think and Grow Rich* as an example. The core message revolves around the power of belief and visualization. If you can envision it and truly believe in it, you can bring it to fruition.

- Then there's Rhonda Byrne's *The Secret*, which popularized the Law of Attraction. Her key message: You must believe your goals are already within your grasp to manifest them into reality.

- Wayne Dyer, in *Wishes Fulfilled*, teaches us to act as if we already possess what we desire. It's about mentally aligning ourselves with our goals, and viewing them as accomplished realities.

- Esther and Jerry Hicks dive deep into aligning your thoughts and feelings with your desires in *Ask and It Is Given*. They explain how belief attracts what you want into your life.

- Joe Dispenza's *Breaking the Habit of Being Yourself* combines science and belief, demonstrating how believing in your goals can rewire your brain to make those goals a reality.

These authors all emphasize the same point: to see your dreams come to life, you must believe they have already been achieved. Transform your wishful thinking into a solid belief, and it will shape your actions and, ultimately, your reality.

I've never been big on religion. Growing up in Denmark, the whole 'God thing' was more of background noise than anything else. Here, discussing faith or religion felt like talking about an old book everyone's heard of but few have read. Yet, I am an avid reader of the Bible. Not for religious reasons, but to understand where all this wisdom originates. Mark 11:24 and Matthew 21:22 both stress that belief in what you're asking for is essential to receive it. Faith and belief are not just spiritual concepts; they're practical tools for achieving your goals.

- Mark 11:24 — "Therefore I tell you, whatever you ask for in prayer, believe that you have received it, and it will be yours."

- Matthew 21:22 — "If you believe, you will receive whatever you ask for in prayer."

So, when I started seeing how much belief plays into success, it wasn't from a place of religious faith. It was more about realizing that whether you're praying or visualizing your goals, the common thread is believing it's already done. Interestingly, the Bible has been saying something similar for ages—believe you've got it, and it's yours. Even without a religious upbringing, I found the connection between belief in achieving goals and what religious texts have been saying quite remarkable.

You must understand that history repeats itself. You must realize that any huge celebrity or successful person will agree with these concepts. If you doubt me, spend a couple of hours on YouTube and see the proof. Successful people talk about this all the time. Even Conor McGregor speaks about the Law of Attraction on a podcast with Tony Robbins. Any Average or Below Average person might claim it's nonsense, but you'll see immensely successful people repeatedly talk about how the way to success starts with complete faith that it is already done.

Muhammad Ali, one of the most celebrated sports figures of the 20th century, famously stated, "I am the greatest. I said that even before I knew I was." Usain Bolt, the fastest man alive, believes in the power of determination and visualization, stating, "I told myself I need to be unstoppable. You need to think about winning, you need to think about being the best." Over and over again, Above Average minds say the same things while Average and Below Average minds reject it as truth. You must learn to think, act, and believe like Above Average minds do. You must choose a side. And yes, there is a side. Unfortunately, the majority of people are raised with an Average mindset. You must study your way out of this. This book contains everything you need. Keep reading.

- Henry Ford, founder of the Ford Motor Company: "Whether you think you can, or you think you can't— you're right."

- Mahatma Gandhi: "A man is but the product of his thoughts. What he thinks, he becomes."

- Albert Einstein: "Imagination is everything. It is the preview of life's coming attractions."

- Walt Disney: "If you can dream it, you can do it."

- Oprah Winfrey: "Create the highest, grandest vision possible for your life, because you become what you believe."

You must choose a side now. The gravity of Average is strong, but you have the power to choose your words, your thoughts, your decisions, your beliefs, your emotional state, and your actions at any given moment. Average and Below Average will pull you down to their level and beat you with experience, while Above Average will let you fly and swim with them in abundance. There is a significant difference between Average and Above Average minds. The biggest difference is that Below Average minds victimize themselves, while Above Average minds take 100% responsibility for their words, thoughts, decisions, beliefs, emotional states, and actions at all times.

Let's now move on to more practical chapters where the rubber meets the road. You're getting closer to the Above Average Method—the method that will set your potential free. This is what you want, and this is what you will get. The Above Average Method will teach you the exact steps on how to do this. But before we get there, let's dive into Part II and talk about the Above Average character. Keep reading!

PART II

THE ABOVE AVERAGE CHARACTER

Part II is a practical section that will help you identify your weakest spots. I won't lie to you. They will be difficult chapters to read if your current mindset is Average or below. You will feel negative emotions because I will guide you to look at yourself for who you truly are, not who you want to be. I will guide you to be honest with yourself. Before you can enter Above Average, you must identify who you really are. You will feel like lying or overestimating yourself. This is normal. This is a defense mechanism all humans possess. We are built to lie to ourselves to feel better about ourselves, but to grow, you must be honest. You must look at yourself in the mirror and face who you are before you can grow into who you want to become. Be aware that your mind will trick you. Your mind will try hard to make you seem better than you actually are. This is a trap. This is what keeps you in the Average or Below Average mindset, but you want to rise above, and for that to happen, you must face what is in front of you with 100% honesty, decisiveness, and courage.

CHAPTER 5

BELOW AVERAGE MIND
AND AVERAGE MIND

"The coward dies a thousand deaths, the brave but one."

- Ernest Hemingway

I will now guide you through practical information and personal development exercises to facilitate your growth. This will be the hardest chapter in the book, so take your time. Reflect deeply. Be honest with yourself, and you will be on your way to Above Average. Do not avoid the pain. Face it. Let's go!

An Average or Below Average mind is reactive, holds fixed beliefs, avoids challenges, focuses on the short-term, and engages in minimal personal growth. In contrast, an Above Average mind is proactive, growth-oriented, embraces challenges, has a long-term vision, and prioritizes continuous personal development. This is exactly what I want you to understand. The information has been available throughout human history. It is accessible now more than ever, so what is keeping the majority from taking it seriously? What is keeping you from adopting it, studying it, and living it? The answer is: your program.

You Must Know What a Below Average Mind Looks and Feels Like

I did not write this book to look down on anyone in any situation. I wrote this book to inspire and inform. I wrote it for those interested in raising their standards and expecting more from themselves. I wrote it for those who want to increase their mental fitness and get what they want in life. Life is a mystery, uniquely designed for each individual, but most people are not designing their lives. They are reacting to whatever happens to them. Think about it for a second. How many of your friends or relatives have said, "I am going to get this, become this, and achieve this by this date," and then followed through? My bet is very few. Why? Because they possess what I call a Below or Average mind.

A Below or Average mind is a mindset that limits individuals from reaching their full potential. This mindset is characterized by a reactive approach to life rather than a proactive one. People with this mindset often settle for what is comfortable and easy instead of striving for what is challenging and rewarding. They tend to follow the crowd, stick to routines, and avoid risks, which ultimately leads to mediocrity and unfulfilled dreams. This mindset is also marked by a lack of vision, where individuals do not set clear goals or have a definite purpose guiding their actions. Instead of viewing obstacles as opportunities to grow, they see them as giant barriers. This way of thinking results in stagnation, halting personal and professional development. This is the harsh truth.

There is a consequence for every choice you make in life. Every action has a reaction. An Average mind is a choice, often an unconscious or misguided one. Whatever mindset you choose to possess will not only affect your personal life but also impact your professional achievements and relationships. People with an Average mind often experience dissatisfaction and regret, feeling they have not lived up to their potential. They struggle with envy and resentment, watching others achieve success and happiness. Do not become like them. This is not a life worth living. You have control. You must lift yourself up from this mindset. You can, and you will!

Below or Average Tendencies

Reactive Approach: A Below or Average mind often reacts to events and circumstances rather than actively shaping their lives. They may feel like victims of their circumstances, blaming external factors for their situation without taking proactive steps to change.

Fixed Beliefs: A Below or Average mind tends to believe that their abilities, intelligence, and talents are fixed traits. They might think success is due to innate talent rather than effort, discouraging them from pushing beyond their comfort zones or trying new things.

Avoidance of Challenges: Facing challenges or stepping into the unknown is often avoided. The fear of failure or making mistakes prevents taking risks, which in turn hampers growth and learning.

Short-Term Focus: There's often a preference for immediate gratification or avoiding discomfort, even if it means sacrificing long-term benefits. This can manifest in procrastination, avoiding challenging tasks, or not setting long-term goals.

Minimal Personal Growth: There is little emphasis on self-improvement or learning from experiences. Individuals may remain stagnant, not developing new skills or expanding their knowledge base.

Identify Your Average Tendencies

My bet is you bought this book because you hope to grow personally and professionally. My bet is that you're interested in achieving more in your life. You wish to unleash your full potential, and to do so, you must identify the current version of yourself to see where growth is necessary. You must confront yourself like never before, bringing forth both your weakest and strongest sides without lying to yourself. Only then can you grow into the person you want to become. Nothing forces you to be the person you were just five minutes ago. You have the power to change everything from this very minute. You can change your entire life in seconds. All it takes is for you to decide! Decide that enough is enough. Decide you no longer want to be held back. Decide to move past your fears, limiting beliefs, and self-pity. No one is coming to save you. No one. But you've heard this before. So why didn't you change? Because of your belief systems. Your program. Your paradigms and self-image.

For change to happen, you must understand where to start and where to go. Your starting point is YOU version 1.0. Your end goal is YOU version 2.0. You version 1.0 is who you are now—the thoughts you have, the words you speak, the beliefs you possess, the decisions you make, and the actions you take. This is not an easy task for beginners, so you must seek guidance from mentors or books. This is why the majority who start their journey to version 2.0 fail and lose motivation shortly after beginning. You will need concrete, simple, and doable things to implement. You need help, and that's what this book is here for. You will need no other books than this one for identifying your version 1.0 and adopting your version 2.0. You will need no more guidance to rise to an Above Average mind other than the Above Average Method and this book. One thing is what you need, another is what you want. You might need further simple and practical guidance, which is why I have created the Above Average Method. Seeking mentors and guidance is positive, so please do so. Let's begin.

Habits - Do this for 14 days straight:

- Find a blank piece of paper.
- Spend a minimum of one hour a day to identify your worst habits.
- When you become aware of them, write them down.
- Write down what triggers your behavior. A feeling. A thought. A friend. A place. A thing.
- Write down how each habit serves you with positive things.
- Write down how each habit serves you with negative things.
- Think no further about it. Just notice and write it down!
- Do this for 14 days.

I will warn you. The Below and Average mindset will in general only do this for a maximum of 10 days. Do not fall into this trap. Do this for 14 days straight. Grow my friend, grow.

Emotions – Now do this for 14 days straight:

- Find a blank piece of paper.
- Spend a minimum of one hour a day to identify your emotions. Feeling happy, sad, irritated, frustrated, fascinated, inspired, fearful, worrisome, angry, disappointed, lonely, joyful, etc. If you lack inspiration of what feelings you have, Google it.
- When you become aware of them, write them down.
- When feeling the feeling, write down what you were thinking of in the moment you felt it.
- After 14 days, summarize the feelings you've had the most.
- List your top five most felt emotions from 1 to 5.
- Think no further about it. Just notice and write it down!
- Do this for 14 days.

The majority of emotions you feel in this period of time equal your quality of life. Is this the life you want to live? Is this the emotion you want to feel? Read this again.

Thoughts – Do this for 10 days straight:

- Find a blank piece of paper.
- Spend a minimum of 10 minutes every day to identify what thoughts you have daily.
- Identify whether they are negative or positive.
- For every negative thought, mark an "X."
- For every positive thought, mark an "X."
- Summarize your total negative and positive thoughts.

- Think no further about it. Just notice and write it down!
- Do this for 10 days.

You have full control over your thoughts. You might just not know it yet. This is what I will teach you. I will teach you the exact method to do so.

Beliefs - Do this for 7 days straight:

- Whenever an opportunity for growth arises, notice what you believe in. Do you believe that you are capable of doing what it takes to harvest the results of the opportunity? Do you believe you are worthy of it? Do you believe you can't, that you are too old, too young, too dumb, or too scared? What do you believe?
- Spend a minimum of 10 minutes every day to identify what beliefs you have daily.
- Identify whether they are empowering or disempowering.
- For every empowering belief, mark an "X."
- For every disempowering belief, mark an "X."
- Summarize your empowering and disempowering beliefs.
- Think no further about it. Just notice and write it down!
- Do this for 7 days.

You have been programmed not to seek out valuable information. You have been conditioned to doubt the wisdom of the best. You have been led to believe you can't succeed. But you can, if you want it. You can, if you truly desire it. You can, if you follow my guidance precisely. You need to do just three things to embed the Above Average mind into your subconscious program:

- Study the information in this book.
- Implement the Above Average Methods week by week.
- Teach the Method to everyone you meet who wants a successful and fulfilling life.

To become Above Average, you must think, believe, and act like an Above Average mind. You need unwavering faith in who you are and what you can achieve. Identify your neuro associations, habits, thoughts, feelings, and beliefs. Recognize that these elements shape your identity and your results. You can change them all to become Above Average. You are nothing more, nothing less than this. You have the power to transform, but it requires effort. Success happens when the rubber meets the road.

Cristiano Ronaldo didn't reach his level of success with an Average mind. Conor McGregor didn't attain his achievements with an Average mind. Oprah Winfrey didn't become a media mogul with an Average mind. Elon Musk didn't innovate across industries with an Average mind. Steve Jobs didn't revolutionize technology with an Average mind. Serena Williams didn't dominate tennis with an Average mind. Marie Curie didn't win two Nobel Prizes with an Average mind.

They chose to transform their inner world. They decided on greatness, starting with their mindset. By now, the Average and Below Average minds have likely given up. They lack the discipline to follow through, but that exercise is your first step to becoming Above Average. Read that again, and then read on.

Refuse to Be a Victim

You must stop seeing yourself as a victim. Most people hold onto a narrative that excuses them from pursuing their dreams. This mindset keeps them from taking responsibility and stepping out of their comfort zones. The result is a life filled with frustration, depression, and a sense of insignificance. When you adopt a victim mentality, you invite more situations that reinforce it. True victims are those physically harmed without reason. For everyone else, your story is in your control. Don't let fear hold you back. Your dreams are within reach if you stop making excuses and start taking action.

Taking responsibility for your life is crucial. Too often, people blame circumstances, upbringing, or bad luck for their situation. Here's the harsh reality: where you are now is a result of your choices. It's time to stop making excuses and start making changes. Your dreams aren't out of reach; you've just been avoiding the effort needed to achieve them. Stepping out of your comfort zone is daunting, and failure is a possibility, but that's how you grow and become stronger. Transforming your dreams into reality requires courage and perseverance.

Think about it. Every moment spent feeling sorry for yourself is wasted time. That time could be spent working on your goals, learning new skills, or taking small steps toward your desired future. The only thing standing between you and your dreams is your mindset.

Decide right now to stop being a victim. Decide not to remain stuck, blaming the world for your problems. Take control, face your fears, and chase after what you want with everything you've got. That's how every successful person has done it. There are no shortcuts. There is no victimhood. It's about what you want and how badly you want it.

Remember, no one is going to hand you your dreams. It's up to you to go after them. The first step is deciding you're no longer a victim of your circumstances but the master of your fate. It's easier said than done, but this is crucial. The Above Average Method will explain the steps in simple terms. This isn't rocket science, but it's hard for the Average mind to break free from its conditioning. You must show up, step up, and reach out for what you want in order to grab it. Not before. Never before.

Let me illustrate with Mariann, a 42-year-old accountant who felt her life was ruined and too late to fix. Read this a few times to see if you relate. Once you do, decide never to be a victim again. It's a decision only you can make, just like deciding what to eat for dinner.

Mariann joined one of my online programs, deeply entrenched in a victim mentality, blaming everything and everyone for her situation. She believed life had dealt her a bad hand, and that was that. Her dreams? Just fantasies, out of reach because the world was against her. She felt she could never do anything right, and when she tried, it seemed like everyone was against her. She had no support from her husband, no one to discuss her goals with, and not enough time to focus on her priorities. She worked on her goals intensely week by week, but somehow, she got distracted, felt unlucky, or refused to persist.

The wake-up call came during an exercise where I pushed her to map out why she had not achieved her dreams. For Mariann, it all came down to a list of blame and excuses. This took place through a simple exercise where I ask my mentees to list their dreams, then list the reasons they haven't achieved them. I then asked her, "What part of this is under your control?"

That hit hard. It turned out that a lot was under her control—way more than she'd ever admitted. She went from an "I can't because..." mindset to one of "How can I?"

That realization flipped a switch for Mariann. She started small, tackling achievable goals, facing one small fear at a time. It was about proving to herself that she wasn't just a passive player in her life story. With each step forward, the old victim narrative no longer fit. It felt foreign, even wrong.

This was not an overnight miracle. But in the process, she did what was needed: she stopped being a victim.

Fast forward, and Mariann is a new person. She's making her dreams real, with plans, actions, and deadlines. One simple realization can transform your life. It is all in your mind.

It's important to acknowledge yourself and clearly see where you have failed in the growth of your mind, your perspective on things, and daily actions. It's crucial to trust the wisdom of history's greatest minds and apply their principles to your life. This can be a daunting task, taking decades to study and apply them all. This is exactly why I wrote this book: to serve you with these principles in an easy and effective way.

Know the difference between the Below or Average and the Above Average mind before you can make any changes. See the difference clearly so that you can stop your Below Average program and work on yourself. Understand the basic principles and start living by them. The next chapter will help to highlight the differences, so keep reading.

CHAPTER 6

THE ABOVE AVERAGE MIND

"Think big and don't listen to people who tell you it can't be done. Life's too short to think small."

- Tim Ferriss

An Above Average mind thrives on challenges, learns from failures, and perseveres in pursuit of its goals. It fosters curiosity, resilience, and the quest for excellence. This mindset understands that abilities and intelligence can be developed through dedication, focus, and consistent effort. It's crucial to realize that "hard work" is a relative term. There's only work you enjoy and work you don't, just like how some games are fun and others aren't. You must learn to love growth. Life is about expansion, and so is the universe. You must expand. Average minds may argue that this leads to stress and depression, but that's a misconception. This belief stems from viewing work as hard and unenjoyable. If you love what you do, think positively, have healthy relationships, and take good care of your body, stress becomes a non-issue. This is a fact.

Above Average Tendencies

Proactive and Purposeful: An Above Average mind actively shapes their life by setting goals and striving to achieve them. They view themselves as architects of their destiny, focusing on what they can control and taking consistent action toward their objectives.

Growth Orientation: They believe in the potential for growth and improvement, viewing intelligence, talents, and abilities as qualities that can be developed through dedication and effort. This fosters a love of learning and resilience in the face of challenges.

Embrace Challenges: Challenges are seen as opportunities for growth. Individuals with an Above Average mindset willingly step out of their comfort zones, try new things, and learn from failures, without letting fear hold them back.

Long-Term Vision: They think strategically about the future, setting and working toward long-term goals. This mindset values delayed gratification, understanding that true success and fulfillment come from consistent effort and patience.

Continuous Personal Development: There is a strong emphasis on self-improvement, whether through formal education, self-study, or life experiences. Continuous learning, self-reflection, and adapting to feedback are essential to their constant evolution and improvement.

Throughout history, you will find philosophers and thinkers with Above Average minds whose ideas and teachings have profoundly impacted human thought and societal development. These personalities didn't just accept the status quo; they questioned, explored, and pushed the boundaries of understanding in their pursuit of wisdom, knowledge, and a better world. From these figures, you can start to learn to adopt an Above Average mind. From these individuals, you can be inspired to take massive action toward your wildest dreams and become the best version of yourself.

Six Notable Figures Who Exemplify the Above Average Mind:

1. Socrates (470–399 BC) – Ancient Greek philosopher who is considered the father of Western philosophy. Socrates, through his philosophical inquiries and the accounts of his dialogues preserved by his students, notably Plato, indirectly taught principles that can be associated with the mindset of winners. While Socrates himself did not explicitly talk about an "Above Average" mindset in the modern sense, his teachings and method of inquiry provide valuable insights into developing a mindset geared toward personal excellence, ethical living, and continuous improvement—qualities often found in successful individuals.

Here are a few key lessons from Socrates that relate to the mindset of winners:

The Importance of Self-Knowledge: Socrates' famous saying, "Know thyself," underscores the importance of self-awareness. He believed that self-knowledge was the foundation of wisdom and essential for living a fulfilled life. For Above Average minds, understanding their strengths, weaknesses, values, and goals is crucial for success.

The Value of Questioning: Socrates is renowned for the Socratic Method, which involves dialogue to stimulate critical thinking. He taught that questioning everything helps individuals reach truth and understanding. This relentless inquiry aligns with an Above Average mindset that values curiosity and learning.

Commitment to Virtue: Socrates emphasized virtues like courage, wisdom, temperance, and justice over material wealth. Winners embody these virtues, leading to personal success and positive contributions to society.

The Unexamined Life Is Not Worth Living: Socrates' statement, "The unexamined life is not worth living," highlights the need for constant self-reflection. For those aiming for success, continuous self-examination is key to growth, learning from mistakes, and making informed decisions.

Admitting One's Own Ignorance: Socrates claimed that he knew nothing, reflecting a mindset open to learning. Recognizing the limits of one's knowledge is the first step toward acquiring more. Winners acknowledge their ignorance, opening the door to new ideas and strategies.

Ethical Living as a Path to Happiness: Socrates argued that ethical living, based on reason and virtue, is essential for true happiness. He believed that immoral actions led to unhappiness. Winners prioritize ethical decisions, understanding that long-term success comes from integrity and positive contributions.

Socrates taught that a mindset focused on self-improvement, ethical integrity, and the pursuit of knowledge leads to true success and happiness. These teachings are relevant for anyone aspiring to cultivate a winner's mindset.

2. Aristotle (384–322 BC) – A student of Plato and tutor to Alexander the Great, Aristotle made significant contributions across various fields, including logic, metaphysics, ethics, politics, and science. His systematic observation and classification methods laid the groundwork for much of Western philosophical and scientific thought.

Aristotle, one of history's most influential philosophers, offered profound insights into human nature, ethics, and the pursuit of the good life, which can be applied to the mindset of winners. Unlike Socrates, who primarily focused on ethical inquiries and the Socratic method of questioning, Aristotle provided a more systematic approach to understanding virtues, happiness, and human potential for excellence.

Here are key lessons from Aristotle that relate to the Above Average mindset:

The Concept of Eudaimonia: Aristotle introduced the concept of eudaimonia, often translated as "flourishing" or "happiness," which he regarded as the highest good for humans. Achieving eudaimonia means living a life of virtue and realizing one's full potential. Above Average individuals adopt this mindset by striving not only for conventional success, but also for deeper fulfillment derived from personal growth and contributing to the well-being of others.

The Golden Mean: Aristotle's ethical theory centers on the "Golden Mean," which asserts that virtue lies between two extremes of excess and deficiency. For example, courage is the balance between recklessness and cowardice. Applying this principle, winners emphasize balance and moderation in all aspects of life, including ambition, risk-taking, and emotional regulation.

Virtue Ethics: According to Aristotle, virtues are developed through habit and practice, not just through knowledge. This suggests that winners are made through consistent actions and the cultivation of virtuous habits such as discipline, perseverance, and integrity. Excellence is achieved through continuous self-improvement and proactive living.

The Role of Rationality: Aristotle believed that rationality distinguishes humans from other animals and that the rational part of the soul should govern the irrational parts. For those striving for success, this highlights the importance of critical thinking, reason-based decision-making, and self-control.

The Importance of Community: While Aristotle's ethics focus largely on individual character and virtue, he also stressed the importance of the *polis* (city-state) in achieving a good life. He believed humans are inherently social beings and that fulfilling one's potential involves active participation in a community. Winners recognize the value of relationships, teamwork, and contributing to the greater good of society.

Teleology and Potential: Aristotle's concept of teleology is based on the idea that everything has a purpose or end goal (telos). For humans, this means realizing one's full potential and purpose. This perspective motivates winners to have a clear sense of purpose and to direct their efforts toward achieving their highest potential.

Aristotle's teachings related to the Above Average mindset emphasize the pursuit of eudaimonia through a balanced and virtuous life, the development of good habits, rational decision-making, and active community involvement. His philosophy suggests that true success is not just about personal achievements but about living a well-rounded, ethical, and fulfilling life.

3. Confucius (551-479 BC) – An ancient Chinese philosopher, Confucius emphasized personal and governmental morality, the correctness of social relationships, justice, and sincerity. His philosophy, known as Confucianism, has profoundly influenced Chinese, Korean, Japanese, and Vietnamese thought and culture. Confucius's teachings provide a robust framework for understanding the qualities and virtues that align with an exceptional mindset—one that strives for excellence and moral integrity.

Here are key aspects of Confucius's teachings that relate to cultivating an Above Average mindset:

The Importance of Self-Cultivation and Continuous Learning: Confucius emphasized the value of education and the ongoing pursuit of knowledge and self-improvement. He believed individuals should constantly strive to better themselves through learning and personal development, a principle central to an Above Average mindset.

Moral Integrity: Confucius taught that moral integrity and virtuous living are crucial for both personal and societal well-being. He stressed virtues such as righteousness (yi), propriety (li), wisdom (zhi), and fidelity to one's word (xin). This ethical framework is essential for anyone aiming to achieve greatness in a manner that is both respectful and beneficial to society.

The Golden Rule: "Do not do to others what you do not want done to yourself." This fundamental principle, advocated by Confucius, is key to developing strong, positive relationships and fostering a compassionate society. An Above Average mindset includes empathy, respect for others, and a commitment to positive social interactions.

The Role of the Superior Man (*Junzi*): Confucius introduced the concept of the "Superior Man" or "*Junzi*," representing an ideal of moral character not based on birthright but on ethical virtue. The Junzi is someone who consistently seeks to improve, behaves according to moral principles, and lives with integrity. Aspiring to be a Junzi reflects an Above Average mindset focused on personal excellence and leading by example.

Leadership and Responsibility: Confucius believed that effective leadership is rooted in moral virtue and the ability to lead by example. He taught that leaders should cultivate themselves morally, prioritize the welfare of the people, and govern through moral example rather than by force or coercion. This approach to leadership underscores the importance of responsibility, compassion, and ethical governance as key components of an exceptional mindset.

Harmony in Relationships: Confucianism emphasizes the significance of harmonious social relationships as the foundation of a stable and peaceful society. This includes respect for roles and duties within families, communities, and the state. An Above Average mindset, according to Confucian principles, involves nurturing positive relationships and contributing to social harmony.

By integrating these principles of Confucianism into your life, you will cultivate an Above Average mind that not only seeks personal achievement and continuous improvement but also prioritizes ethical integrity, compassion, and a commitment to the greater good. Confucius's teachings inspire us to pursue a path of moral excellence and leadership that benefits both ourselves and society.

4. Earl Nightingale (1921-1989) – An influential American radio speaker and author, Earl Nightingale was a pioneer in the personal development industry. His most famous work, *The Strangest Secret*, encapsulates his philosophy on success and the power of mindset.

Nightingale's teachings offer valuable insights into cultivating an Above Average mind.

"We become what we think about." This is the core of Nightingale's message in *The Strangest Secret*. He believed that the quality of our thoughts directly shapes the quality of our lives. An Above Average mindset is consistently focused on positive, constructive, and ambitious goals. Nightingale suggested that by directing our thoughts toward our desired outcomes, we initiate the process of becoming what we aspire to be.

Here are some key ideas from Nightingale that relate to the concept of an Above Average mindset:

The Importance of Goal Setting: Nightingale emphasized the significance of setting clear, precise goals. He argued that without specific goals, individuals cannot harness their full potential. An Above Average mindset involves not only dreaming big but also setting actionable objectives and working persistently toward achieving them.

Taking Responsibility: Nightingale advocated for personal responsibility in achieving success. He believed individuals must take charge of their lives and decisions. According to him, an Above Average mindset means refusing to blame circumstances or external factors and instead taking full responsibility for one's destiny.

The Value of Continuous Learning: Nightingale was a strong proponent of lifelong learning and self-improvement. He encouraged reading, listening, and absorbing new information as a way to grow continually. This dedication to learning and personal growth is a hallmark of an Above Average mindset.

Service to Others: Nightingale believed success comes from providing value to others. He taught that contributing to others' success and well-being brings success back to you. This principle reflects an Above Average mindset that looks beyond personal gain to making a meaningful difference in others' lives.

Positive Attitude Toward Failure: Nightingale viewed failure not as a setback, but as a crucial stepping stone to success. He believed that each failure teaches a valuable lesson, bringing us closer to our goals. Embracing an Above Average mindset means seeing failure as an integral part of the learning process and using it to propel oneself forward with renewed determination.

Earl Nightingale's teachings on the power of positive thinking, goal setting, personal responsibility, continuous learning, service to others, and resilience in the face of failure provide a comprehensive blueprint for developing an Above Average mind. He taught that success isn't the result of luck but the natural consequence of consistently applying these principles.

5. Jim Rohn (1930-2009) – An American entrepreneur, author, and motivational speaker. Rohn significantly influenced the personal development industry. His teachings and philosophies on success, habits, and personal growth have inspired millions to pursue excellence and develop an Above Average mindset. Rohn's approach to personal development and emotional fitness centers around several core principles.

Here are some key ideas from Jim that relate to the concept of an Above Average mindset:

The Philosophy of Personal Responsibility: Jim Rohn stressed the importance of taking responsibility for one's life, circumstances, and happiness. He believed individuals have the power to transform their lives through their actions, decisions, and attitudes. This principle is foundational for an Above Average mindset, promoting self-reliance and proactive behavior.

The Power of Goal Setting: Rohn emphasized that setting clear, specific, and achievable goals is crucial for success. He advocated writing down goals and developing detailed plans to accomplish them. This practice helps individuals focus their efforts, stay motivated, and make steady progress toward their desired outcomes.

The Role of Habits and Discipline: According to Rohn, our daily habits shape our future success or failure. He emphasized the importance of developing disciplined routines and making consistent, incremental improvements. Rohn's famous quote, "Success is nothing more than a few simple disciplines, practiced every day," encapsulates this concept.

The Value of Lifelong Learning: Rohn was a strong advocate for continuous personal and professional development. He encouraged reading, attending seminars, and seeking mentorship as ways to expand knowledge and skills. Rohn believed that self-education and a commitment to learning are key drivers of success and personal fulfillment.

The Importance of Time Management: Rohn taught that time is our most valuable asset, and that effective time management is crucial for achieving success. He recommended prioritizing tasks, focusing on high-value activities, and avoiding procrastination to maximize one's time.

The Significance of Relationships: Rohn highlighted the impact of relationships on personal and professional success. He famously stated, "You are the average of the five people you spend the most time with." This principle emphasizes the importance of surrounding oneself with positive, supportive, and inspiring individuals.

The Practice of Financial Wisdom: Rohn emphasized the importance of developing financial discipline, investing in assets, and creating multiple income streams. He stressed living within one's means, saving a portion of earnings, and learning to manage finances wisely.

Jim Rohn's teachings on personal responsibility, goal setting, discipline, continuous learning, time management, the importance of relationships, and financial wisdom provide a complete blueprint for developing an Above Average mindset. His legacy lives on through his books, seminars, and the numerous individuals and leaders he has influenced, inspiring them to pursue excellence, make significant changes in their lives, and reach their full potential.

6. Robert Kiyosaki (1947) – The author of *Rich Dad Poor Dad* underscores the importance of financial education, investment, and understanding the difference between assets and liabilities as essential to achieving financial independence and wealth. While his book mainly addresses financial literacy and entrepreneurship, many of his principles can be applied to developing an Above Average mindset, particularly in terms of financial success and personal growth.

Here's what Mr. Kiyosaki says that relates to an Above Average mindset:

Financial Education Is Key: Kiyosaki emphasizes the critical role of financial education in achieving success. He argues that understanding how money operates and learning to make money work for you are essential. An Above Average mindset requires a commitment to learning and mastering financial principles and strategies.

Mindset Over Money: Kiyosaki often states that it's not the amount of money you have that makes you wealthy; it's your mindset and knowledge of how to use that money effectively. He advocates thinking like the rich, which involves understanding and leveraging investments, real estate, and businesses to build wealth.

Assets vs. Liabilities: A core teaching of *Rich Dad Poor Dad* is the distinction between assets and liabilities. Kiyosaki advises people to accumulate assets—items that put money in your pocket—over liabilities, or items that take money out. An Above Average mindset involves making informed, strategic choices to grow your asset base over time.

The Power of Entrepreneurship: Kiyosaki believes entrepreneurship is a powerful vehicle for financial success and personal growth. He encourages taking calculated risks, starting businesses, and investing in oneself. Developing an Above Average mindset means being proactive, innovative, and willing to step outside your comfort zone to reach financial goals.

Overcoming Fear and Taking Action: Fear of losing money is common, but Kiyosaki teaches that fear should not paralyze you. Instead, use it as a motivator to become more educated and make smarter decisions. An Above Average mindset involves confronting fears, learning from mistakes, and persistently moving toward your financial objectives.

Creating Multiple Streams of Income: Kiyosaki advocates diversifying income sources through investments, real estate, and businesses. An Above Average mindset is about not relying on a single source of income (like a salary), but instead, building multiple streams that can lead to financial freedom and wealth.

Giving Back: Beyond personal wealth, Kiyosaki highlights the importance of giving back and using wealth to positively impact others and society. An Above Average mindset includes recognizing the broader role of wealth in contributing to the well-being of others.

Robert Kiyosaki's approach to an Above Average mind is deeply rooted in financial intelligence, entrepreneurship, and the courage to act on one's knowledge. He teaches that by adopting the right mindset and continuously seeking to improve one's financial education and actions, achieving wealth and financial independence is within reach.

★   ★   ★

You have the resources to achieve everything anyone else has or ever will accomplish. It is never about the lack of resources; it is your mindset and resourcefulness.

- Learn to understand this and refuse to become a victim.
- Learn to decide what's right in any situation.
- Recognize that the right thing is almost never the easiest one.
- Learn that mental pain is an illusion.
- Realize that your dreams will only come true when you commit to the work it requires.
- Accept that victimhood does not exist when it comes to reaching your goals. Show up, step up, and do what is needed.

This is the only way. This you will learn in the Above Average Method once you go all in. Keep reading.

CHAPTER 7

DECIDE TO GO ALL IN

"Work like there is someone working 24 hours a day to take it all away from you."

— **Mark Cuban**

Going "all in" isn't merely a phrase; it's a wholehearted commitment to your dream, a willingness to risk everything for what you believe in. It means not holding back, not waiting for the ideal moment, but plunging headfirst into your goals with all your energy. Let me share a personal story to demonstrate this.

When I launched miinto.com, it was just an idea—a dropship solution for small stores without an online presence. At the start, we had nothing tangible to offer these shop owners: no website, no visitors, just a contract and a vision. However, I believed in this vision with every ounce of my being. So, I went all in.

Every day, from 10 a.m. to 8 p.m., for six long years, I visited shop after shop. I encountered rejection, skepticism, and numerous obstacles. It was an unrelenting grind, a test of determination, but my commitment never wavered. Why? Because going all in means more than just hard work; it's about perseverance, unwavering belief in your vision, and the relentless pursuit of your goals. Remember, I wasn't born with exceptional skills. I wasn't born into wealth. I came from a working-class family with a father who was severely mentally ill and a mother who fought for our survival. I developed an Above Average mind just like you are doing now. If I could do it, so can you.

My journey with miinto.com wasn't just about building a successful platform; it was a testament to what "all in" truly means. It's about putting all your cards on the table, betting on yourself, and overcoming every challenge—not for days or weeks, but for years, if necessary.

Going all in with something you're passionate about will undoubtedly yield great results over time, but be mindful as you progress. You need to love what you do. You need to infuse passion and desire into it, but your mindset along the way is crucial for your well-being. You can't go all in for a prolonged period without any breaks. You need to slow down at times and attend to your physical and mental needs. You need pit stops. You need strategies to maintain your pace, or eventually, you will burn out. I burned out. I know what it feels like to hit the wall of stress. I also know what caused it. It wasn't that I went all in; it was that I went all in with too many tasks I disliked. This is why I wrote this book—to teach you how to adopt an Above Average mind without compromising your health, your relationships, and your family. Most people fear going all in. They fear the pressure, and there will be pressure, but diamonds are formed under pressure, and so will you be.

You must recognize the power of your own decisions. Understand that every choice you make today shapes your tomorrow. What you decide to eat for dinner becomes your body. What you decide to do now impacts your future. Realize that waiting for the perfect moment is a surefire way to stay stuck. Then, take action, even if it's small, to move closer to your goals right now and every day from now on.

Decide what you want and what you are going to do about it. Know why you want it—it must be so compelling that you can't stop waking up thinking about it. Become obsessed with getting what you want and face your fears every day until they become nothing. Fear is only fear until you confront it. If you're afraid of doing something, do it afraid (Will Smith). It's only your mindset holding you back. Only! Nothing else is stopping you. Think about it for a moment. What do you want right now that you have tried to get, and what stopped you? Conclusion: your attitude, your limiting beliefs, your thoughts, feelings, and habits. That's it. "All in" means what it says: ALL IN!

The Above Average mind doesn't choose to go all in; they are all in by nature. This has become their way of living, a part of their subconscious program. You can do this as well. It's simply about training the mind, understanding the difference, and testing your comfort zones often enough. The fear of the potential pain of going all in on something is much greater than the actual pain. Your anticipated fear is always bigger than the reality. When expecting a slap on the chin, the fear of the slap is always worse than the actual slap. Not that it doesn't hurt, but the anticipated pain is bigger. You must learn to accept that nothing grows without pain. Nothing. "All in" is your highway to growth. The all-in mentality is part of the Above Average mind.

Let me illustrate this with something relatable: weight loss. Almost everyone tries to lose weight at some point in their lives. Going all in here doesn't mean just cutting back on the occasional soda or hitting the gym once in a while. It means completely transforming your lifestyle. It means deciding enough is enough. It means getting the results you want. It means searching for all available information to understand the process of weight loss. You seek mentors, coaches, or knowledge in books. You have no cheat days since the word "cheat" doesn't belong in going all in. You don't crave sugary, fatty, and calorie-dense meals. You're committing to regular, consistent exercise—not just when you feel like it, but when you have planned it. It's about setting clear, achievable goals and tracking your progress, ensuring every meal and every workout counts. It's not just a diet; it's a new way of living.

This is ALL in—an absolute commitment, not a half-hearted attempt. Whether it's weight loss, starting a business, or any other goal, it's about putting in the work day in and day out, not just dipping your toes in the water. It's diving headfirst and not looking back. It's about going all in with things you love to do, all day, every day, for the rest of your life. All in.

Throughout this book, when I say, "you must," it's not just advice; it's a blueprint for turning your dreams into reality. You must be willing to commit fully and believe in your vision, even when it seems like the world doesn't. That's what it means to go all in.

You Must Set and Work with Goals

Setting and working with goals is essential. You need to realize that goals direct your focus. When you are clear about what you want, you instruct your subconscious mind to guide you toward that specific target. People with an Average or Below Average mind often focus on what they lack, what scares them, or the negatives in their lives. This negative focus signals the subconscious mind to attract more of those thoughts. What you think is what you perceive. It's like programming a GPS with the wrong destination and then wondering why you never get where you wanted to go.

You must aim for big goals. Those who advise you to set small, easily achievable goals are often profiting from the notion that success is simple. It is not easy, but it is worthwhile. You must expand your imagination and push yourself beyond your comfort zone. You need to believe these goals are already within your grasp. When you have unwavering faith in your goals, you send a powerful command to your subconscious mind. It begins working tirelessly to align your actions and decisions, presenting you with opportunities to achieve those goals. It supplies you with the ideas necessary to reach your objectives. You must start living intentionally rather than reactively. When you determine precisely what you want and when you want it, you begin to move toward it. It's not magic; it's human capability. It's what every human is capable of but the majority (Average minds) have been brainwashed into believing they cannot. You must understand that the capitalistic system prefers doers over thinkers. Provide a concrete argument for why you cannot become a multimillionaire—a factual one, not based on fear.

Explain factually why you cannot achieve it. If you have two hands, two ears, one mouth, two legs, and a brain, what separates you from a multimillionaire? Your thoughts, beliefs, decisions, and actions. That's the only difference. Another undeniable truth!

You must understand that setting goals is a way of living. You either do it consciously or unconsciously. Your subconscious program (your paradigm) already has clear goals. It already knows what it wants, but it has not been designed by you. Your program already directs you toward something, but is that something you truly desire? You might always look for jobs with a minimum salary. You might always seek the easy way out. You might always find yourself in destructive relationships. You might always seek as much comfort as possible. You must understand that you have the power to rise above your environment. You can think about what you think about. You can accept or reject ideas. You can act even if you don't feel like it. This is the power of humans. Focus on your goals as already accomplished. It's not just about aiming high; it's about firmly believing that you're already there and then working backwards to make it your reality. This is how it's done. This is how Michael Jordan did it. This is how any self-made billionaire did it. This is how any top athlete did it. This is the way.

You have unlimited potential and everything at your fingertips. You must start to set goals that inspire you—goals that you desire and goals that frighten you. You must start doing this now.

You must set and work with goals in the right way. The right way is the only way. The Above Average Method will teach you exactly how to do it. One thing is to make a list of what you want and then make a list of everything you must do to make it happen. Another thing is to actually do it. This is your inner world—your thoughts, beliefs, emotions, emotional states, decisions, and actions. I don't teach my mentees to set goals. I teach them to set goals and believe they are already achieved. This is how they succeed. This is the inner world. It is always your inner world that creates your outer world—your results. Even if you are born with a physical disadvantage, you can accomplish anything you set your mind to. Anything.

- Consider Stephen Hawking. Despite being diagnosed with amyotrophic lateral sclerosis (ALS) at the age of 21, a condition that gradually paralyzed him, Stephen Hawking went on to become one of the most renowned theoretical physicists in history. Hawking didn't let his physical limitations confine his intellectual pursuits.

- Or look at Nick Vujicic. Born without arms and legs due to a rare disorder called tetra-amelia syndrome, Nick Vujicic has become a global inspiration as a motivational speaker and author. He founded Life Without Limbs, an organization that helps people find hope and meaning. Nick's message focuses on overcoming obstacles and living a life without limits, demonstrating that physical disadvantages do not define one's ability to achieve great success and make a significant impact on the world.

- Or what about Wilma Rudolph? Wilma Rudolph overcame childhood polio and physical disability to become one of the world's fastest women. At the 1960 Olympic Games in Rome, she became the first American woman to win three gold medals in track and field during a single Olympic Games.

They all went all in. They all worked with goals. They all embody the Above Average mind. At this point, you should feel very motivated. If not, start from scratch with the book again. Do not keep reading. Start over and study what I am writing. By now, anyone who understands what I am writing will feel highly motivated. This is the moment you begin to realize that you have unlimited potential. Congratulations. If so, you are moving into the Above Average mind. Your journey has just begun.

You Must Understand Fear and Laziness

You must understand that you are the only object standing in your way of achieving your goals. Your mind. Only your mind. Rudolf Steiner, a philosopher and mystic, identified these as the twin barriers to our greatest selves. Let's break this down. The two colossal walls standing between you and your heroic potential are fear and laziness. That's it. Understand that when you choose to follow the directions of your fears, it is inevitable that you will end up disappointed. It is a guaranteed lose-lose scenario.

Take a moment right now to reflect on what you want to achieve in your life. Picture the best version of yourself. Now ask yourself:

- How does that person look?
- How does that person think, talk, and act?
- How much does that person earn?
- How does it feel to be that person?

Can you see it? Can you feel it?

If not, write the descriptions of that person down on paper and read it aloud to yourself until you start feeling it. Now, ask yourself: *What's stopping me from closing the gap between who I am and who I want to be?* If you're brutally honest, you'll find that external obstacles aren't the real issue. Rather, it's your internal ones—your own fear and laziness. Your inner world is Average or Below Average. You must decide to focus on becoming the best version of yourself. Visualize that person as often as you can. To be someone, you must become someone, and it starts from within. It begins with your thoughts and mental images.

Above Average minds don't just have strength—they have strength for two. Their secret weapon is love. Yes, love. They are willing to fight for those they love. They do what they do to help others more than just helping themselves. They have a bigger purpose. They see their personal development (awareness expansion) as a tool to be better for everyone around them. The Average mind would classify this as egocentric behavior. It is anything but that. Above Average minds know that they have the power to help those around them, and this fuels even more passion, willpower, determination, and perseverance within them. So, ask yourself, for whom are you willing to give up your fear and laziness? For whom will you dig deep and give everything you've got? Who matters most to you, and what life would you like to give them?

I'm here, committed to refusing to listen to my fear and laziness for my family, friends, team, and community. Setting and working toward big goals isn't just about my personal success. It's about overcoming the fears and laziness that hold me back from achieving extraordinary things, like Stephen Hawking, Nick Vujicic, and Wilma Rudolph did, despite their physical challenges. They didn't let fear or laziness dictate their future. They focused, believed in their goals as if already achieved, and moved beyond Average. It's simple, but not easy.

You must understand that any drama in your life is just mental drama. There is no real drama. There is nothing dangerous unless you are in a life-threatening situation. There is nothing to fear. You won't die from failure. You will learn from it. In fact, you must fail, and you must fail fast, hard, and often. The difference between those who succeed and those who fail is that the successful ones give it one more effort until they succeed. They failed just as much, if not more. But they tried again, and then again. It is not about how hard you can get hit; it is about how high you bounce back when you hit the ground (Rocky Balboa). Failure is learning. No one with an Above Average mind has never met failure. Not one!! Everyone who has ever surpassed Average has tasted failure. Without exception. You must accept this truth to succeed.

- Steve Jobs got kicked out of Apple, the very company he created. But he didn't give up. He bounced back, founding NeXT and Pixar, then returned to Apple and changed our world with the iPhone.

- J.K. Rowling heard "no thanks" from publishers a dozen times before Harry Potter saw the light of day. A single mom with no money, fighting depression—she lived through the hardest circumstances imaginable. Yet, she didn't let go. Her pile of rejections became the stepping stones to her becoming the author of the best-selling book series in history. She holds the world record for book sales in 24 hours—11 million copies!

- Or what about Walt Disney? He was told he lacked imagination and had no good ideas, then watched his first company crumble. Imagine that—Walt Disney, out of ideas? But yet, he proved them wrong, creating a legacy that redefined entertainment. Disney's early flops are proof that your biggest failures can lead to your greatest achievements if you just keep going!

Failures are your lessons, and they're non-negotiable on the road to success. They are a must-experience part of the journey. You must endure failures before you can succeed. It's an essential part of the process. So, your fear of failing is the mental drama blocking you from ever achieving success. Read that again.

You must conquer fear and laziness to rise to an Above Average mind. When you do, you not only achieve your goals but also inspire those around you to strive for their best. It's about more than just personal achievement; it's about the impact you can make when you're at your best. So, who are you doing this for? What are you going to do? Go!

You Must Commit to Mental Training

Understand and learn to develop and expand your inner world. You live in two worlds: your outer world, which includes your results, and your inner world, which encompasses your thoughts, beliefs, emotions, emotional states, decisions, and actions. Mastering your inner world is essential to creating whatever you desire in your outer world.

Mental training is like hitting the gym for your mind. You need to do it regularly, put real effort into it, and set a consistent schedule for your sessions. Think of it as an appointment you can't miss. After finishing school—whether high school, college, or university—most people stop learning. They stop picking up new books and making any effort to sharpen their minds. This is where they go wrong. Your strength, kindness, emotional health, dreams, beliefs, and fears all start and end in your mind. You are as emotionally fit as you have been programmed to be until you start developing your emotional fitness. Dr. Jordan B. Peterson often discusses this.

If you're not actively working on your mental fitness, you're letting your most powerful tool get rusty. Imagine if you stopped walking or moving entirely; your physical muscles would weaken over time. The same goes for your mind. Without consistent mental exercise, your ability to think, solve problems, and manage emotions diminishes. This understanding is not common among Average or Below Average minds. They go day by day, doing the same things repeatedly, reacting the same way, and seeing the same results, all without incorporating mental training into their lives. They then blame external factors for their failures. This is living in denial and leads to self-pity.

You must engage in mental training with the same dedication as a professional athlete trains their body. This means setting aside time each week, committing to learning and growing, and challenging your mind with new ideas, perspectives, and skills. Your mind is the control center for everything you do, feel, and achieve. Remember, you're only as capable, compassionate, and mentally fit as the effort you put into training your mind. Don't let your mental muscles weaken. Train them. Grow them. It's all in your mind—your dreams, your beliefs, your fears. Everything.

Cristiano Ronaldo exemplifies someone who doesn't just rely on physical abilities but also dedicates significant effort to mental training. His success on the soccer field is as much due to his mental strength as it is to his physical skills. Ronaldo's approach to mental training is disciplined, focused, and as rigorous as his physical training regimen.

Ronaldo incorporates visualization techniques into his routine, imagining himself scoring goals and executing perfect plays before stepping onto the pitch. He also practices mindfulness and meditation to maintain his mental health, manage stress, and sharpen his concentration. Ronaldo understands, like any other Above Average mind, that being mentally present in the game allows him to react swiftly and make smarter decisions under pressure.

Ronaldo is renowned for his unwavering self-belief. He sets high goals for himself and firmly believes in his ability to achieve them. He envisions his success as already achieved. He comprehends the power of the subconscious mind. He personifies an Above Average mind. The Above Average Method will guide you through the exact steps needed to train your mind. Keep reading!

You Must Commit to Being a Role Model

Understand that the people who inspire you are role models for millions. Learn to become like them. Study what they have done to inspire you and others. Do the things you say you want to do. The greatest paradox in humanity is the fear of failure, yet those who inspire us the most are the ones who fail and come back stronger. Even small actions can inspire others.

Let's say you want to go from earning $50,000 a year to $200,000 a year. You step up, start reading books, invest in mentors, make plans, prioritize your weeks, and take daily actions. You decide to make it happen. You face your fears, fail, and learn from your mistakes until you reach your goal. You will inspire people. It's that simple. This is the only way to become a role model for many. There is a formula to get what you want in life, just as there is a formula to make a great lasagna, run a profitable hair salon, or grow a fast-paced SaaS company. All you need is the formula and the mindset to do it.

Understand that Average and Below Average minds will try to drag you down. The more you grow, the stronger the pull, until it snaps like an elastic band and they all turn into fans. Many people I've met on my path to inner greatness asked why I do all this and why I try to be someone special. The same people now ask me how I did it. This book is for them. This is why I wrote this book—to help them, too. Inside, they all want to achieve great things but are too scared to try, so the easiest way to feel good about themselves is to make you conform. Do not fall into this ego trap. Do not listen to them. Think about it. I have never met a highly successful person who told me to give up my dreams, who said I shouldn't think I was special, or that I shouldn't strive to be someone I am not. A highly successful person would encourage me to continue and achieve my dreams just like they did. This clearly differentiates Average and Above Average minds.

In Denmark, we have something known as *Janteloven*, or the Law of Jante. It's a set of principles that essentially says you shouldn't think you're special, better, or smarter than others. It promotes humility and equality, but in reality, it paralyzes ambition and individual achievements, discouraging people from standing out or believing in themselves to be better versions of themselves.

Here are the ten rules as traditionally listed:

1. You're not to think you are anything special.
2. You're not to think you are as good as we are.
3. You're not to think you are smarter than we are.

4. You're not to convince yourself that you are better than we are.

5. You're not to think you know more than we do.

6. You're not to think you are more important than we are.

7. You're not to think you are good at anything.

8. You're not to laugh at us.

9. You're not to think anyone cares about you.

10. You're not to think you can teach us anything.

This is what Denmark has deeply integrated into its culture. Do not listen to this ridiculous law. I do not fall into this trap. I never did and I never will. This book is written to show you the way to being Above Average and to not be like everyone else. This book is written to challenge what the majority believes. This book is about the science of achievement.

You Must Invest in Mentors (Yourself)

The majority of people have been told a lie—a lie I was told as well. I was told that information is power, but it is not. Information without action is meaningless. Jim Rohn, a mentor to extremely successful people like Tony Robbins, once said: "Don't let your learning lead to knowledge, or you will become a fool. Let your learning lead to action, and you become wealthy. There is nothing more pitiful than a guy who is smart and broke." Only with guidance from those who have taken the road to riches or success themselves will you learn the exact way to achieve your dreams. They know the way!

It's crucial to find the right mentors and invest in them, or rather, invest in yourself. Understand the three pillars of achievement and put everything into action. The three pillars of achievement, inspired by Tony Robbins, are:

1. Focus
2. Best Strategies
3. Align Inner Conflicts

First, focus on what you want. Then, acquire the best insights, the best knowledge, the best strategies, the best mentors, and the best books. Align your inner conflicts and understand that only resolving them will lead you to the results you desire. One inner conflict could be wanting to become very rich but fearing judgment from others. You must choose your side, as you can't have both in the real world. It could also be wanting a deep and loving connection with your partner but fearing getting hurt, feeling insecure, or being lied to. You must align these conflicts and face your fears to get what you want. Do not follow the directions of your fears.

This is essential to achieving your goals. Information alone won't get you anywhere. It's like having a map but never taking your first step. Without applying what you learn, knowledge remains just potential energy, untapped and ineffective. Jim Rohn's advice isn't just a catchy quote; it's a fundamental truth. Knowing a lot but doing little with that knowledge leads nowhere. It's action that transforms your life, not the mere accumulation of facts. Being the smartest person in the room means nothing if you're not using that intelligence to achieve your goals. I have never completed any public education, yet I've held seminars in front of people who have. I've even conducted seminars at universities. Think about that for a moment.

Finding mentors who have traveled the path you're on is invaluable. They offer not just advice but actionable insights, drawn from real experience. They've navigated challenges, faced setbacks, and emerged victorious. Their wisdom isn't theoretical—it's practical, tested, and proven. I have invested hundreds of thousands of dollars in my own knowledge, mindset, and personal development. I've read more than 600 books about human behavior, successful people, and basic psychology. I've worked with several mentors, some well-known and others not. I allocate 3% of my income to a personal development account every month. When you invest in yourself, it's like receiving a stock certificate in yourself. This becomes your certificate of confidence and commitment to constantly strive toward the Above Average mind.

You must be willing to listen and then act on the advice given by your mentors. It's not just about finding someone successful and absorbing their wisdom. It's about taking that wisdom and applying it to your journey. This is how you avoid being "smart and broke." It's how you turn potential into reality. You must invest in mentors. Seek out those who have achieved what you aspire to achieve. Learn from them, but more importantly, apply what they teach you. This isn't just an investment in their knowledge; it's an investment in your future. Remember, the Above Average Method provides exactly that, so congratulations on already making this investment. Let's learn how to tap into your personal power in Part III. Keep reading!

PART III

PERSONAL POWER

By now, you've laid the foundation. I have instructed you on your inner and outer worlds. The mastery of your inner world isn't just theory; it's the practical skill set for this section. Mastery of your inner world, as I've explained, isn't merely academic; it's the essence of the transformative journey you are on.

In Part III, you will learn the true power of your mind, crafting mental pictures that not only inspire but also ignite the reality you want to see in your outer world. You must believe it before you see it. You must feel it before it shows. Mental pictures will make you feel it. Mental pictures are the foundation of all feelings. The Average mind will find it hard to unleash the power of their mind simply because they are often filled with anger, jealousy, cynicism, and egoism. These are not just emotions; they are blockers to your growth. Nothing has ever grown in a negative environment. Nature does not thrive in a negative environment. Animals do not survive in a negative environment. Humans do not grow in a negative environment.

PART II

PERSONAL POWER

CHAPTER 8

UNDERSTANDING YOUR PERSONAL POWER

"Your thoughts become your words. Your words become your behavior. Your behavior becomes your habits. Your habits become your values. Your values become your destiny."

- Mahatma Gandhi

It all starts in your mind—your internal dialogue and thoughts. Like a beacon, they signal to the universe your deepest desires and fears. It's a simple equation: negative thoughts attract negativity, while positive thoughts attract possibilities and joy.

Your transformation does not stop at your thoughts. It extends to your attitude, which serves as your blueprint for how you see the world. When you shift your attitude, you shift your life. You must understand that everything is energy. Move away from the Newtonian materialistic worldview and accept the latest quantum science proving that everything is energy. Let me explain.

Is the human body made of cells, atoms, or molecules? To answer this, let's start with larger structures and work our way down. The human body is composed of many things covered in skin. Focusing on the skin for a moment, what is it made of? The simple answer is skin cells. While I'm ignoring the complex structures and levels of skin for simplicity, other structures are similar: muscles are composed of muscle cells, bones of bone cells, nerves of nerve cells, etc.

We know the body is made of cells. What are cells made of? Cells consist of proteins (a type of molecule), water (another molecule), and other components, all made of molecules. At the center of the cell are DNA and RNA, both extremely complex molecules. So, cells in the body are made up of molecules. What are molecules made of? Molecules are collections of atoms. Water is made up of oxygen and hydrogen atoms. Proteins are made of carbon, hydrogen, oxygen, and other elements. Thus, the molecules making up the cells of the body are composed of atoms. In the end, it is correct to say the body is made of cells, molecules, and atoms.

Learn to dance with energy. You must understand that whatever you are feeling is vibrating at a certain frequency. Positive emotions vibrate at higher frequencies, while negative emotions vibrate at lower frequencies. In this dance of energy, what you give out returns to you tenfold. Good luck and good wishes are not just gifts to the world; they are investments in your own future, cultivating a garden of abundance that thrives on gratitude. Gratitude itself becomes a key player for your emotions and, thereby, frequencies. You must understand that thoughts and emotions release chemistry in your body. Your mind constantly sends signals to your body depending on the situation. Every cell in your body has an electromagnetic field around it. Whatever feeling you have, your mind sends a signal to your cells via electrical impulses to either grow or protect themselves.

When you're feeling negative emotions, your cells will protect themselves and cannot grow. The emotion of fear releases stress hormones in your body, causing your cells to react with protection. In protection mode, your cells cannot maintain themselves, and your immune system weakens. This happens through electrical signals in split seconds. The new cell biology theme, epigenetics, confirms this truth.

New science has shown how thoughts and emotions release electromagnetic waves, measurable with a MEG device. This is not philosophy; this is science. Leading cell biologists know about this. Bruce Lipton, a cellular biologist best known for his groundbreaking stem cell research at Stanford Medical School and his work in epigenetics, has emphasized how behavior and environment can affect gene functioning. The concept that our thoughts can influence the physical world has often been denied in scientific discourse, tracing back to the 17th century when René Descartes introduced the notion of dualism, separating mind and matter. The idea that one's beliefs could impact physical health has traditionally been dismissed as wishful or magical thinking. Dr. Bruce Lipton himself has encountered skepticism toward these views. However, he points out that contemporary scientific research firmly supports the interconnection between the mind and the body.

Lipton highlights that it's not just the chemical composition of our bodies that affects cellular function but also electromagnetic energies and the subconscious mind. He criticizes the traditional Western scientific approach for often ignoring the importance of energy in health, citing challenges in measurement and quantification as reasons for this oversight. Despite evidence that energy fields can impact living organisms, these findings are frequently dismissed by the scientific community due to a lack of a clear explanation of the mechanisms involved.

Lipton asserts that energy plays a crucial role in regulating cellular activities. He explains that electromagnetic frequencies and patterns influence every biological process, from DNA activity and cell development to neural growth and hormone production. This understanding is why treatments like electroconvulsive therapy (ECT), which apply electrical currents to the brain, can be effective for certain mental health conditions, demonstrating the significant impact of energy on cellular and physiological functions.

Recognize that you have the power to change your thoughts, emotions, and thus the frequency in your body that either heals or harms you. You possess unlimited potential; you just might not realize it yet. You have the ability to heal yourself. You have the capability to make things happen. You have the power to alter your thoughts, emotions, actions, and consequently, your life outcomes. This section will teach you how to tap into this power. Enjoy!

You Must Learn to Master Mental Pictures

I have explained enough for this to make sense. I've told you about your inner and outer worlds and the importance of mastering your inner world. This section is about exactly that. First, you must understand that everything you do is because you've seen it in your mind first. I call it your mental eye. Some call it the third eye, but to avoid confusing or deep spiritual terminology, I'll use a more relatable term. You must understand that your mind thinks in pictures or movies. Think about it for a moment. Recall a time when you felt really good. Do it now. What do you see? What do you hear? Do you play a movie, or do you see a picture?

Most likely, both memories and feelings came to mind. This is your mental eye at work. Whatever you see in your mind, combined with thought and emotion, your subconscious mind takes as truth and signals the body via electromagnetism. Let's say you start worrying about paying your bills. This will trigger an emotional response that releases stress hormones in your body just from the thought.

Your subconscious mind controls everything happening in your body without your conscious awareness. I explained this earlier in the book—your cells' communication, your heartbeat, your breath, your blood flow, your hormones. Everything. Now, understanding this, my example will make more sense.

Consider this. Have you ever tried gaming with a virtual reality device? I assume yes or that you at least know about it. If yes, have you ever tried one of these games where you are in a scary environment? It could be on top of a skyscraper, in a zombie apocalypse land, or a war zone. Have you noticed how your entire body reacts when you play these games? Your hormones get fired up, your fear, cortisol, adrenaline, and everything gets activated. This is the power of mental images. Whatever you see in your mind in mental movies that you entertain intensely enough, your subconscious mind will react to as the truth.

I will give you another example. Have you ever suspected that a coworker might be undermining your project based on overheard snippets of conversation or incomplete email threads? What did you visualize with your mental eye (mental pictures or movies)? The scenarios you willingly (though perhaps not consciously) played in your mind triggered your subconscious mind to accept them as truth. Perhaps you imagined situations where this person criticized your work to others or manipulated decisions behind your back. You started feeling mistrustful, anxious, or even hostile toward your coworker. Then, when you finally addressed the issue by having a direct conversation, you discovered that your coworker had different perspectives or information but no malicious intentions. Have you ever experienced that? This illustrates the power of your subconscious mind. These mental pictures are what you must learn to master.

Shaping Your Reality

Mastering mental pictures is a crucial skill for shaping your reality. The images you create in your mind—those vivid, emotion-packed movies—set the stage for what manifests in your life. Think about it for a moment. The last time you were completely convinced and had full faith in getting what you wanted, how did you go about it? You were filled with confidence and determination. You took massive action and found a way. I'm not saying you just imagine what you want, add faith, and then it falls into your lap. No, it starts with that vision, and from there, the path is built. You move confidently toward your dreams. You see failures as learning opportunities. You embrace and trust the process completely. To achieve what you want, to embody confidence, to fuel your motivation and inspiration, and to feel unbreakable, you must master your mental pictures. You must see your end result not as a wishful dream but as a dream already accomplished. This isn't about hoping; it's about believing with unshakable conviction that what you seek is already yours. This will take practice, and this is what I will teach you.

When you have complete faith in your vision, it instructs your subconscious mind to guide you toward realizing it. Ideas will come to you unexpectedly. This is what I call infinite intelligence. Remember, the question is never *how* you'll achieve your desires. The "how" will come to you, but only when you know precisely what you want and why you want it, combined with complete faith that it's already done. It is yours to take. Understand that your subconscious mind does not question or doubt; it operates based on the certainty of your beliefs. Just like any other extremely successful athlete or person. Whoever you research will tell you the same thing. They believe it before they see it. Spend some time searching for it online, and you will find my words to be true. This is the Above Average mind. This is what I will teach you in the Above Average Method later in the book.

Mental pictures are your secret weapon. You must learn to direct and control them, commanding the universe, or as I refer to it: infinite intelligence. The same intelligence that created one cell from another and then constantly multiplied into your being. Who controlled that process? Some call it God; I call it infinite intelligence. The same intelligence scientists have studied for decades and continue to study intensely. You must fill your mind with images of your victories, your joy, and your achievements as if they are happening right now. With this practice, you're not just dreaming; you're actively creating the life you want, guided by the unstoppable force of your belief. When you master your inner world, you will achieve everything you desire.

Let Go of Anger, Jealousy, Cynicism, and Egoism

The Average mind is fueled by jealousy, insecurity, and anger. I'm not writing this to hurt anyone; I am writing this to make you aware of the majority's mindset—a mindset doomed to failure. It has never been and will never be possible to build a meaningful and abundant life with a mind fueled by negativity. Some might achieve temporary success, but it won't last. History repeats itself. Egoism, greed, cynicism, jealousy, and anger have done nothing but harm the world. These emotions can drive our motivation, making it easy to fall into this trap. But I am here to tell you to let go of these feelings starting now. This is not easy, but it is possible. Some people master this, but most don't. This is what creates peace, love, and harmony in the world. When humans start to love unconditionally and understand there is more than enough for all of us, everything changes. All war is built on these negative emotions. All pain stems from them, and ultimate failure is inevitable when fueling your mind with these concepts. I can only write this because I have been a slave to these emotions and these destructive thoughts and behaviors myself.

In 2023, I had the profound experience of undergoing a so-called "Ego death." I will tell you the story, but you may find it hard to understand how it works. You have to experience it to fully grasp it. I do not recommend anyone to do the same, but it was a mind-blowing expansion of awareness for me.

I was invited by my mentor, Klaus Veile, to his house in central Denmark. I flew from my home in the south of Spain to spend the day with Klaus and a few of his so-called "magic workers." I had a one-hour body therapy session, a one-hour energy healing session, and spent three hours talking with Klaus afterward. It was incredibly emotionally challenging, and I cried for hours but left feeling lighter when I returned to Spain.

The next day, I invited my loving girlfriend to join me at our favorite beach club, where we usually spend our weekends enjoying the sun, fresh fruits, and delicious green smoothies. As

I lay in the sun, completely relaxed and almost drowsy, my sub-conscious mind brought forth a memory from my childhood. I experienced it in first-person view as if it were happening in the present moment. I remembered how I felt as a child, with all the sounds and surrounding conversations just as they were back then.

As children, we do not have the conscious understanding or desire to listen to other conversations. We just exist, completely observing without judgment. I was filled with extreme peace. I do not remember the last time I felt like this. Suddenly, I was hit by a cruel, anxious feeling that grew within me. I felt on the verge of a panic attack, but something in me dared to just "go with it." So, I did, and on the other side, my Ego died.

My conscious mind returned, but this time I was free of any negative emotions. There was no noise, no judgment, and ideas came to me like never before. I could see (mentally) clearly, and everything made sense. I had no hate, no anger, no anxiety—nothing but extreme happiness, the same happiness we experienced as kids. I could sense when I felt like judging something or someone, but I could choose whether to do so or not. I was on the "other side," as they say in spiritual terms. My Ego was dead, and I started creating a greater meaning for my life. Life is about joy and harmony. Everything is in harmony when we arrive here. The rest we learn to feel. In this state, my creativity increased a hundredfold, and I noted down many things I have since worked on applying in my life. This book is the result of that experience. In that state, egoism, greed, cynicism, jealousy, and anger did not exist. This is why you have to let go of these emotions. Without them, there would be no mental disorders. Read that again.

Before this experience, I had worked on myself a lot, par-ticularly my emotional and spiritual well-being. The first time

I read *Think & Grow Rich* by Napoleon Hill, I did not study it. I merely read it without truly understanding it, but I did take something into my life. I read a section where Hill instructed me to suggest the following to myself for at least 30 days straight. This had a huge impact on my life, and I advise you to do the same. He instructed me to read the following out loud to myself twice every day:

I know that I have the ability to achieve my definite purpose in life, therefore I demand of myself, persistent, continuous action toward its attainment and I here and now promise to render such action. I fully realize that no wealth or position will long endure unless it is built upon truth and justice; therefore I will engage in no transaction which does not benefit all to whom it affects.

I am succeeding by attracting to myself the forces I wish to use and the cooperation of other people. I induce others to serve me because of my willingness to serve others. I eliminate hatred, envy, jealousy, selfishness, cynicism, anger, and fear by developing a true love for all humanity, because I know that a negative attitude toward others will never bring me success. I cause others to believe in me because I believe in them and believe in myself.

This is my creed, my quest. To never stop striving for the top. To always keep moving forward. To always be the very best I can be. I am the power. I am the magic. I cannot be stopped. I am a winner. I promise to always be true to myself because I am the creator and master of my universe and I am responsible for making a positive difference in the world and to the quality of life in it. I live in constant and never-ending improvement.[1]

And so, I did as the book instructed, and the results have been incredible.

Learn to let go of things. Find your true inner peace and understand that without egoism, greed, cynicism, jealousy, and anger, you will rise to the Above Average mind. This is especially true when you understand the power of your thoughts. You will receive precise instructions on how to do this in the Above Average Method. Keep reading.

---

[1]

CHAPTER 9

YOU MUST UNDERSTAND
THE POWER OF THOUGHTS

"You have power over your mind - not outside events. Real-ize this, and you will find strength."

— Marcus Aurelius

You hold complete control over your thoughts; they are yours to change at will. Yes, at will. However, much like habits, changing thought patterns isn't an overnight task. You must understand that your 86 billion neurons have constructed "highways" of thought patterns, along which your mind sends thoughts as if cruising on a German autobahn.

Just like habits, your thoughts have their own routines. Think about it—someone walks in and reminds you of someone you didn't like in the past. Instantly, your brain goes, "Great, another one," or "This is going to be annoying." It's quick, automatic, and happens without you even trying. It occurs unconsciously.

But have you ever tried talking with this person only to realize they're nothing like the person you remembered? Turns out, they're actually pretty cool, and you find yourself enjoying the conversation. Most of us have experienced this, which is a clear example of how habitual thoughts operate. Learn to actively choose to question and go beyond your automatic thoughts and take control. Your thoughts significantly impact your reality. They influence your emotions, decisions, and ultimately, the course of your life—your destiny.

People with Average and Below Average minds have little to no idea about this. They do not understand that we have the power of our thoughts. They do not know that most of our thoughts have been programmed into our minds since childhood. I wrote about this in Part I. I explained where most of our thoughts and beliefs originate. This you must understand, and this you must master.

Let me give you another example from my own life. I was raised by my mother. My father has suffered from mental illness for as long as I can remember, which eventually led to my parents' separation. My mother has a very narrow vision of how things work, what is right, and what is wrong. Do not misread this—I love my mother. She has given me all my strengths and also weaknesses, just like any parent does to their children. But I've expanded my awareness to realize that most of my beliefs were false. Any limiting belief is false. There are no such things as limitations, except physical ones as far as we know from physics.

Albert Einstein shattered physical limitations, setting new boundaries. Limitations are merely mental constructs. Everything in life is governed by math; we just haven't figured it all out scientifically yet. My mother believed starting your own business was risky and that it was difficult to succeed. She's a driven, formidable woman, and if she believed in her potential, she would move mountains. However, her belief in the risks and difficulties influenced me. It made me fear starting my own business, focusing on everything that could go wrong, the security I could lose, and the potential financial failure. But this was and is a misconception. I've proven that wrong many times. I've built five multimillion-dollar companies, and everything I've touched has turned into success. Some ventures are bigger than others. Don't get me wrong—I have met failure on my journey to success, but no one can stop me from trying again. Keep trying until it works, and you will succeed.

The fact is, your thoughts control your emotions. Your emotions control your actions, and your actions create your results. From my NLP Master Diploma, I learned this process happens in a split second. Even now, while you're reading this, your mind is making choices. First, your mind decides what to focus on, either consciously or unconsciously. Then it assigns a meaning to it. Depending on the meaning, it triggers positive or negative emotions, which lead to action or reaction. Assign an empowering meaning to something, and it changes the game. Assign a disempowering meaning, and it's game over.

Two people, same age, same fitness level, same education, but different upbringings, will end up living completely different lives. Why? Because of their thoughts and beliefs. To change your life, you must first change your thoughts. Your thoughts determine your focus and the meaning you assign to things or situations.

I was coaching a 37-year-old woman aiming to lose 25 kg to return to her physique from her 20s. As a single mom with a seven-year-old daughter, she received everything needed to succeed—a personalized workout and diet plan, daily support from me and my team, plus all the facts on calories and weight loss, and daily motivation. We knew our program worked; our high ratings from hundreds of clients proved it. Yet, after three months, she had gained weight instead of losing it. But then, something changed.

One morning, while driving her daughter to school, her daughter, looking out the car window, turned to her mother and said, "I wish it was you who ran with me to school while I was on my bike, Mom…" That moment transformed everything for her. It changed her perspective (her thoughts) on weight loss and created a powerful new motivation. Suddenly, losing weight wasn't just about aesthetics; it was about being active and present for her daughter. That shift in thought led to her losing 20 kg in just four months. This illustrates the power of your thoughts and the meaning you give to situations. This you must learn to master. This I will teach you.

You must understand that your thoughts are the blueprint for your actions; change the blueprint, and you change everything. Recognize that any successful person owes their success solely to the thoughts they cultivate daily. You must realize that you can change your thoughts whenever you choose. If you're bombarded by negative thoughts, reject them and replace them with positive ones. Initially, this is challenging for the Average mind since they are programmed to think in terms of fear, losses, and worries. A trained mind will follow the patterns it has practiced persistently over time. Now, you might wonder how you've been trained in these negative thought patterns. One source of daily training is the news you consume. While most journalists are good people, they operate in a capitalistic race for readership. The more readers they attract, the more money they make, and what attracts readers are disasters, wars, and drama. Think about it for a moment.

How much drama did you read or hear in today's news? It's no secret that the news industry thrives on people's fear. Fear attracts readers, and fearful news generates negative thoughts.

Begin the journey of reprogramming your thought patterns by becoming aware of your thoughts. Pay attention to your habitual thoughts and question their validity. Are they serving you, or are they holding you back? From there, consciously choose thoughts that align with your goals and the person you aspire to be. With time and practice, you'll find your mental pathways leading you to places you once only dreamed of. The Above Average Method will teach you the techniques to do so. Keep reading.

Change Your Attitude to a Positive One

I will keep this section short and straight to the point. When-ever you've met someone with a positive attitude, how did that make you feel? Good or bad? If it made you feel bad, it is because you were jealous of this person's outlook on life. It is not possible to envy someone with a positive attitude. It is not possible to dislike someone with a positive attitude. It is not possible to lose in life with a positive attitude. Failing in life is inevitable, but losing in life means failing without ever cor-recting your mistakes. This will lead to self-pity, anger, jealousy, and egoism.

Human beings are the only species on Earth aware of our own mortality. Yet, we live as if we will never die. We act as if we will always have the physical and mental energy we do now, but we won't. At some point, certain things will become physically impossible for us. At some point, it will be mentally exhausting to do simple tasks we could easily handle in our 20s and 30s. You must understand that you won't be here forever. You must realize that the only things you take with you to your grave are your memories and regrets. Life is about expansion. Nature is about expansion. Life is about expanding our awareness, and the only way to do this is by weakening our ego. Our ego obstructs growth. It can be a great motivator initially, but it is not a good long-term leader.

In 1956, a groundbreaking audio recording was released by American radio host and motivator Earl Nightingale, whom I consider the "Godfather" of the self-help industry. He spoke extensively about attitude, the magic word that creates our best positive actions, sensations, and emotions. You must understand that your attitude has significant power over your success and outcomes.

You are a spiritual being, and your thoughts, emotions, and actions are interconnected. A positive attitude leads to positive outcomes, while a negative attitude results in negative outcomes. William James, an influential Harvard professor, observed that people can change their lives by altering their mental attitudes. Various laws, like the Law of Cause and Effect, govern our lives, and by living according to specific principles, you can guarantee success. It's pure science. Creating results has a clear process, a process you must learn to follow. Each result you desire has a written process behind it; therefore, it is science. Hence, everyone can achieve their ultimate goals.

Neville Goddard, a significant 20th-century author, introduced the Law of Assumption, which explains how your assumptions and beliefs shape your reality. Your life is the drama you assume it to be. Assume the worst for your day, and your mind will make it so. You must understand that your brain is on a mission to prove your assumptions right, no matter how wrong they might be. This you must learn to accept.

Understand that your mind and body work together to create your life's outcomes. Thoughts lead to emotions, which lead to actions, which in turn lead to results. Therefore, if you want to change your results, you must change your thoughts, emotions, and actions. Adopt a positive attitude toward every situation and person you meet. This is what the Above Average mind does. This is what you must do as well.

Your attitude toward yourself and the world significantly impacts your life. A poor attitude toward yourself often leads to a poor attitude toward others and attracts negative experiences. You must adopt a good attitude, expect the best, and you will receive exactly that: positive experiences and the best outcomes. Successful people (Above Average minds) expect more good than bad from life and believe in themselves. They see success as the natural outcome of their actions. They have complete faith in themselves, and what they touch turns to gold. Your world mirrors your attitude. If you wish to change your surroundings, you must first change your attitude. Poor attitudes can cost us jobs, promotions, and even marriages. You must adopt a successful attitude before you can transform your life. You are what you think about all day long. This too the Above Average Method will teach you. This too you shall learn. Keep reading.

Express Goodwill, Good Wishes, and Gratitude

If you want to be popular, you must be likable to people. You must understand that popularity comes when people like you. People like those who have a positive attitude, look up to others regardless of success level, encourage others to do better without judgment, help others without expecting anything in return, show genuine interest, kindness, and willingness in every situation, listen more than they talk, offer support rather than criticism, and spread positivity rather than negativity.

Don't focus on becoming popular, but focus on doing what it takes to be likable. Decide from today that you will do exactly what I tell you to do. When you do, you will become popular, achieve incredible results, and live your most passionate life. If you want to be successful, you must be successful with people. Your success will depend on the value you provide to others. Your success depends on your attitude. Your success depends on your willingness to grow into a better person. Grow into a confident person. Grow into a giving person. Grow into a loving and caring person. Grow into an effective person. In business, your success depends on how people respond to you. One of my mentors taught me these principles. One of my mentors was Mr. Kopmeyer. I do not take credit for all my knowledge. I just share with you the knowledge I've acquired throughout my lifetime. I have had dozens of mentors. I was not born with this knowledge. You are not born with this knowledge. To be someone, you must become someone. To become someone, you must define what that "someone" is and then go out and be it. There is nothing stopping you from being different from who you were five minutes ago. You can use your will to become whoever you want to be. You have full control over your thoughts, emotions, and actions. This requires training and understanding.

If you want to be happy, you must be happy with people. To become popular, successful, and happy, you must be liked by people. To be liked by people, you must first like yourself. To like yourself, you must speak, think, and act positively. A good place to start is by following Mr. Kopmeyer's "3 G's":

Always express:

1. **Gratitude**
2. **Goodwill**
3. **Good Wishes**

These 3 G's will give you all the happiness and success you can imagine. These 3 G's should be written on all surfaces you visit often to remind you of them until they become an integrated part of your identity. This will take time. Change takes time. Give it time. You must, without exception, always follow these three principles whenever you are with other people and learn the power of emotions. The Above Average Method will teach you precisely how to do it. Keep reading.

CHAPTER 10

YOU MUST UNDERSTAND THE POWER OF EMOTIONS

"Emotional self-control—delaying gratification and stifling impulsiveness—underlies accomplishment of every sort."

- Daniel Goleman

How you're feeling dictates your actions or reactions in every moment. Your emotions are the control center of your behavior. Every day, your emotional state determines the actions you will take. Emotions are not just feelings; they are the driving force behind your actions. When you feel good, you're likely to tackle big projects or hit the gym with ease. When you're feeling down, even small tasks can seem insurmountable. You have complete control over your emotions, as they are driven by the mental pictures or movies your mind chooses to focus on. Whatever your mind is watching will spark an emotional response.

There are only two major emotions: Fear and Joy. The rest are segments that fall under these two categories. Fearful/negative emotions could be anxiety, panic, dread, insecurity, worry, nervousness, terror, apprehension, desperation, jealousy, or paranoia. Joyful/positive emotions could be happiness, contentment, excitement, elation, gratitude, optimism, satisfaction, amusement, love, or pride.

Mastering your emotional state means mastering your mental pictures or movies. You have complete control over your mental pictures or movies. But like anything else, gaining this control will take persistent practice. Your emotional state is the boss of your actions. Accepting this will give you an edge— the ultimate edge. You can start taking charge of your emotions instead of letting them take charge of you. You must learn to change how you feel. It is easier than the Average mind thinks. It is hard at first, but when you persist and practice the demanded techniques daily, it will become an automated thought pattern like anything else in your life. Tying your shoes was hard at first. Driving your car was hard at first. Kissing your first love was hard at first. This is the law of life. Everything new is hard at first.

One of my clients had an experience where his emotions took over and got out of control. He was in a relationship with his girlfriend for five years. Both were hard workers. He was an accountant and a lawyer. Every day his girlfriend would be home around 6 p.m. for dinner. If she was late, she would either call or text him to say she was coming late. Then one day, she did not come home at 6 p.m. Martin wondered why, and when the clock hit 7 p.m., without hearing anything from his girlfriend, his thoughts started playing tricks on him. He first got worried that something had happened to her. Around 8 p.m. his thoughts started panicking, but now his thoughts had changed from worry to anxiety. Maybe she was with another man. Maybe she was tired of him. Maybe she was tired of him not changing his behavior after all the talks they had had. Maybe she was cheating on him. By 9 p.m. he was furious. His mind started ensuring conspiracies of who she was with and where they were. He was mad. Really mad. His emotions were angry, insecure, filled with a sense of injustice and frustration. When the clock hit 9:45 p.m. and she came in without having responded to any of his 37 text messages and 25 calls, he met her at the door full of those emotions, only to realize she had been in a traffic accident.

Your memories of the past can play tricks on your future visions. Learn to master these emotions by promoting new narratives—better narratives, positive narratives. Every second of your day, this process happens in your mind: Focus - meaning - emotion - action - result. First, your mind decides what to focus on. Second, it decides what this means to you, which activates an emotion. That emotion promotes an action that leads to an end result. Either you take control over this process consciously, or your autopilot (subconscious mind) will do it for you. Give something an empowering meaning, and it changes the game. Give something a disempowering meaning, and it is game over.

You have the power to give things an empowering meaning. You have the power to create positive emotions that promote positive actions and results. In the above example with Martin and his girlfriend, his autopilot took over and resulted in a painful cascade of negative emotions, which he met his poor girlfriend with at the entrance. If Martin had taken control over the meaning of why his girlfriend did not answer the calls, he would have been able to meet her with compassion, care, and love when she entered. You must understand that the meaning you give things or situations creates positive or negative emotions that lead to positive or negative actions, which lead to positive or negative outcomes.

Here is another example. One of my clients had been struggling with her economic situation for many years. She was a single mother to her eight-month-old son and had never had a job where she earned decent money. She could barely afford my online program but decided to give it a try. On the onboarding call with one of my team members, she was asked, "What do you really want?" She could only answer with very vague goals that clearly had a negative meaning behind them, so she never truly believed she could achieve what she wanted. When we asked her what was holding her back from going for one of her goals—writing a book about being a single mom—she answered, "I don't think I can write a book." My client was clearly filled with fear and negative thoughts about herself. Her self-belief was at rock bottom, so we told her about how similar her story was to that of J.K. Rowling, who faced numerous rejections and hardships before *Harry Potter* became a global phenomenon. Rowling, however, chose to give her failures an empowering meaning. Instead of seeing rejections as a sign to give up, she viewed them as steps closer to success, a testament to her perseverance and belief in her story.

The turning point for my client came when we shifted her perspective, inspired by stories like Rowling's. She began to see her struggles not as barriers but as unique content for her book, giving her the push she needed to start writing. This change in meaning transformed her actions, filling her with a newfound sense of purpose and positivity. Instead of being held back by the fear of failure, she was driven by the possibility of sharing her story and inspiring others.

Giving an empowering meaning to your challenges changes everything. You hold the power over your emotions, and the Above Average Method will teach you how. Keep reading.

Increase Your Awareness

While awareness has often been discussed in the spiritual sector, I am here to tell you that you are a spiritual being. I was never a believer in spirituality because my understanding and judgment of it were flawed. I assumed spirituality was only for spiritual people. The Average and Below Average mind might agree with my younger self. But this is not true. We are all spiritual beings with consciousness. You must accept yourself as a spiritual being. When you search for the definition of "spiritual," it says: "relating to or affecting the human spirit or soul as opposed to material or physical things" or "relating to religion or religious belief."

This is not the complete meaning of spirituality. Often, what science has yet to prove is labeled as spiritual. Not everything unproven by science is spirituality, but much of it overlaps. Science and spirituality have much in common. Both focus on life and our existence, the universe, our place in it, matters related to birth and death, evolution, and the nature of reality or truth.

Rakhi Roy Halder says: "'Self' is a form of energy. We use the term 'Potential of the Self' quite frequently. But have you ever thought about where this potential comes from? Why are extraordinary little ones found in different parts of the world who know such things, which are impossible to tell at such a tender age? Every matter in this world is made of atoms. In a matter, one or another atom's nucleus is deteriorating with time. In this way, time affects matter. Our body is a matter, but the 'Self' is a form of energy. Time can't affect the 'Self.'"

Dr. Bruce Lipton says: "The moment you change your perception is the moment you rewrite the chemistry of your body. Becoming aware of the subconscious source of our behavior gives us an opportunity to change our lives by rewriting the programs of limitation or the things that interfere with us. If we change those programs, we are empowered; free to express the wishes and desires of the conscious mind. This is really what the whole new biology is all about. Take us away from, 'You are a victim of life,' to introducing the fact that we are the creators of our life. Our consciousness is the source of the great potential of creating heaven on Earth."[2]

Let go of the victim story you tell yourself and embrace the new science of epigenetics—the science of mind over genes—to regain power and create the lives we want. You must understand that you have the power to change your life completely by thinking differently. Learn to increase your awareness to identify your negative thoughts, impulses, reaction patterns, and emotions.

Increase your awareness in any situation you possibly can. The more aware you are, the less irrational you will be. Irrational people do not master their emotions. Irrational people do not get what they want. Irrational people often possess an Average mind. Humans in general are not rational at all—we are governed by our emotions. Therefore, you must learn to master your emotions, reactions, impulses, and your emotional self.

Becoming rational requires deep work and training. You may think you are in control, but you're not. We are born irrational. To become rational, you must train to be rational. The journey is not just about understanding others; it begins with self-awareness and understanding yourself. Increase your awareness

2

and understand that altering your attitude and approaching people with a more open spirit will transform your life. This is guaranteed. Learn to become independent and think for yourself. Gain control of your emotional responses. Being rational means being aware of your irrationality. It means being aware of the emotions that govern your decisions, your negative thought patterns, your bad habits, and your inner world. You can only be aware of yourself, not of others. You're not aware of how other people perceive you.

You're often stuck in your own tunnel vision of your thoughts and preoccupations. You must stop reacting and adopt a more detached view of life. What makes you react all the time is that you're locked inside yourself—you're not paying attention to others or to your own emotions. Understand that you can't succeed in this world if you're bad with people. One of the most important decisions in your life is who you choose to partner with—who you choose to keep very close to you. We often make the worst decisions in these areas because our decision-making is clouded with emotion. You must respond to people as they ARE, not as you want them to be.

Some of the greatest leaders in history were rational people—Marcus Aurelius, Queen Elizabeth I of England, Abraham Lincoln, and Nelson Mandela. To develop your awareness, you must have the right tools. These tools will be provided to you in the Above Average Method. Keep reading.

Identify Your Ultimate Goal

I've experienced a wild life, a calm life, an outrageous life, a party life, a successful life, a poor life, a rich life—every kind of life, but always MY LIFE. The majority of people do not live THEIR LIFE. They live A LIFE, but not THEIR LIFE. The Above

Average mind lives THEIR LIFE. You can only live your life if you know exactly what you want your life to be about. Nine out of ten people, if asked about their top three goals for the next month, will give vague answers. Answers that prove they haven't given it much thought. They weren't taught this in school and often haven't considered it. Goals are something they know about but never act upon. They've thought of goals but only as wishes. A goal and a wish are two completely different things. You can't have a goal of wanting to win the lottery—that's a wish.

You can't have a goal of simply wanting more money—that's a wish. You can't have a goal of wanting a better relationship—that's a wish. A goal is specific, measurable, achievable, relevant, and time-bound (SMART). To identify your ultimate goal, you need clarity. It's about defining exactly what you want, ensuring it matters to you, and setting a deadline. You must learn how to set goals to rise above Average.

For example, instead of wishing for "more money," set a specific goal like "increasing my monthly income by $500 within the next six months through freelance projects." This isn't just about desire; it's about planning. It involves creating a strategy, taking action, and establishing criteria for success.

Identifying your ultimate goal requires deep introspection. Ask yourself why you want what you want. The "why" will drive you, especially when times get tough. It serves as your motivation, your reason to keep going when everything else tells you to stop. You must identify an incredibly motivating reason why. If your "why" is weak, your persistence will be weak. If your "why" is not deeply rooted in your desire, your discipline will crumble.

Let me explain. Imagine I lay a wooden plank on the ground, 10 meters long, just wide enough to walk across by placing one foot in front of the other. I offer you $500 to walk from one end to the other. You'd probably jump at the chance—easy money, right? Now, take the same plank and imagine it stretched between two skyscrapers, 100 floors up. Cross it, and you get another $500. Most would say no way. And that's a rational decision.

But here's where it gets interesting. Picture someone you deeply care about on the opposite skyscraper, with the building on fire, and crossing that plank is the only way to save them. Would you do it then? For many people, the answer turns to yes. What changed? The risk, the height, the danger—they're all the same. But your "why" shifted dramatically. It became powerful and undeniable. This is a strong "why." You must learn to identify "why's" as strong as this example to get what you truly want in life.

Above Average minds set goals for what they truly want in life. They do not hold back. They know what they want, they know why they want it, and then they take massive action until they get it. They see the goal as already achieved and live each day as if the goal is theirs. They do not stop for anything. You must learn to identify your deepest desires. You must learn to set goals for yourself, but not just any goals. You must know what you truly want in life and do everything you can to get it. Average and Below Average minds do not do this because they don't know how to achieve their deepest desires. Therefore, they do not want to disappoint themselves and turn toward becoming like everyone else. The gravity of Average is strong. It feels much easier not to go for what you want in life. The fear of failure and being judged is significant. You must learn to defy that fear. Fear is just an illusion, a belief you've been programmed with. The paradox is that those we admire the most in the world are often those who fail and come back stronger. Failure is a part of the journey. You must fail to learn. The Above Average mind knows this; the Average mind does not.

You must ask yourself often: "What do I really want?" You must focus on your deepest desire every day. You must develop an undeniably strong "why." Why must you achieve this? Why is this important to you? Why must you do this? You must turn your "should-do" into "MUST-do." This is why my book is filled with MUST DO. You must do what I say and exactly what I say to achieve your wildest dreams. This is not philosophy; this is what Above Average minds do every day. You are not born Average. You are born unique. You are born a genius. I know this from a study conducted by George Land and NASA.

George designed a test to pinpoint when a genius emerges. They evaluated 1,600 children aged four and five, and astonishingly found that 98% of these kids were deemed geniuses based on the test results. This was a remarkable discovery, so they decided to test the same group later in life. By the time the children reached school age, only 30% still scored as geniuses. By high school, that number had dropped to just 12%. The most disheartening result was that as adults, only 2% were classified as creative geniuses. In other words, we are educated out of our natural genius as we grow up. This means we ARE geniuses inherently; you simply need to have unwavering faith in this. You are initially programmed by infinite intelligence to be a genius but later conditioned to believe you are not. You become what you believe. Your ultimate goal in life is within your grasp. You must identify it and take massive action toward it every single day.

You Must Evaluate Yourself Often

A life not evaluated is a life destined for any destination but your own. Learn to design your life the way you want it. Here's a simple fact: You will end up at an end destination either designed by you or by others. The majority of people go to work every day, waiting for Friday to come. They work not because they love what they do but because they need to make enough money to experience a tiny bit of freedom. You must understand that humans are not made for work. Work is made for humans. Capitalism switched this around and schooled us to believe we could become something great.

The reality is that the majority of people do not achieve greatness, at least not in terms of living the life of their dreams. Most humans work until they are 65 years old, then go on a so-called pension where freedom finally exists. You must understand that a life where a vacation is needed is not a fulfilling life; it is a job. A job that serves a bigger purpose for someone who enjoys freedom every day. Above Average minds do not have a job; they have a mission, a goal, a passion, and a purpose. You do not need to become an entrepreneur for this, but true freedom only exists where you do not need a vacation from work. "Work" is a job. "Passion," on the other hand, is a lifestyle you do not want freedom from.

Once, someone asked me, "Mike, when do you plan to retire and stop working?" I smiled and explained that it would be like asking me when I would stop playing as a young child. My answer was never. I never want to stop playing. My life is my game—a game designed by me. This is freedom.

Above Average minds do something special: they take time every week, at least 1-2 hours, to closely examine their lives. They think about how they are doing, what they are learning, and what they have accomplished. Then, they figure out how to improve from there. Self-evaluation is like a bridge that helps you move from who you are now to who you want to be. It's not about being hard on yourself; it's about understanding what you're good at and what you need to work on. Then, you use what you learn to grow, step-by-step. Average minds will say you are a perfectionist.

Above Average minds will say you are smart. Most people have never spent even five hours evaluating themselves, their lives, their goals, their relationships, their finances, their mindset, their physical health—everything. This is not rocket science; it's simple. In school, teachers evaluated you to let you know where to improve. This is exactly the same with your life. Your life is more important than school exams. You only get one life, but most people act as if they will live forever. That's why they drink excessively every weekend, take drugs, never work out, and over-eat. You must understand that your body is the house of your soul. Your soul cannot function without it, nor can it achieve your ulti-mate goals in life if it is in bad shape, sick, and tired. To improve, you must know where to improve. To improve, you must know what to improve. To improve, you must evaluate yourself and your life. The Above Average Method will teach you this as well.

You have reached the end of Part III. The time has come to put all the knowledge you've studied into practical action. As I told you at the very beginning of the book, you must do only three things to install the Above Average program into your subconscious mind:

- Study the information in this book.
- Implement the Above Average Methods week by week.
- Teach the Method to everyone you meet who wants a successful and fulfilling life.

By now, you have all the information you need to rise Above Average. Now, it is only your will that needs to be used. If there's something you still don't understand, go back and read the book again. I suggest you read this book every month for at least 12 months while you implement the Above Average Method. Every time you read and reread, the information will be programmed into your subconscious mind, and the Above Average Method will become second nature. You must understand that the Above Average mind has internalized everything in this book. It is only when it becomes a part of your subconscious mind that the Above Average Method will fully work. Some of it might work, but to get what you want in your life, you must study until it is part of your subconscious program. It has to be known. It has to be a part of you. To be someone, you must become someone. You can only become what you believe you already are. To believe in something, you must repeat things in your mind over and over again. You must practice opening the gateways to your subconscious mind. This is what hypnotherapy does. This is what will happen when you read, study, and teach the writings in this book.

Good luck!

PART IV

THE ABOVE AVERAGE METHOD

Welcome to Part IV, the section where everything you've learned transforms into real action. This is where you'll start doing things differently, using your new knowledge to change your life. It's all about integrating the Above Average way into your everyday routine.

You've acquired the knowledge, and you're ready to change. Now, it's time to make those changes happen. This part of the book is your guide to implementing the steps that will elevate you to Above Average and help you achieve everything you want in life. Make no mistake—you must follow all the steps to succeed. Some steps might challenge you. This is good. Some steps might come easily. This is also good.

Learn to say: "This is good" to everything. This is the mindset of Above Average minds. This is the attitude you will need to propel you forward.

CHAPTER 11

THE ABOVE AVERAGE METHOD - STEPS 1 TO 10

The Above Average Method focuses on the following three principles:

1. **Doing Things:** You will take weekly actions to integrate the Above Average mind into your day-to-day life. Small daily steps will make a significant difference.

2. **Building Thoughts:** You are what you think all day long. New thoughts foster new actions, which lead to new results. This is the only way to create lasting change.

3. **Teaching What You Learn:** Understanding deepens when you teach others. Share your journey and the Above Average ideas with those around you. Teaching isn't just about helping others; it strengthens your own understanding as well.

You must accept that becoming an Above Average person doesn't happen overnight. It takes time, effort, and stepping out of your comfort zone. As you work through this part, keep an open mind and stay committed. Things won't work unless you work for them. Dedicate yourself to these principles for at least 12 months. You will receive a detailed manual on how to do this when you sign up on my website.

Let's begin the journey.

Step 1: Identify Your Ultimate Goal

First things first, you must identify your burning desire or your ultimate goal. This isn't about a simple wish or a hopeful dream. It's about a compelling, grand desire that consumes you. Whether it's financial independence, more freedom, or a happy family life, it must be something that ignites a fire within you. It must be something you truly want, something you don't yet know how to achieve but desire deeply anyway. It must be a goal that makes you doubt if you can achieve it, something bigger than anything you have ever thought you were capable of accomplishing. It cannot be vague. It must be a pulsating, vibrant yearning—a definitive goal that channels all your thought energy, all your strength, and all your effort. When you think about achieving it, you should smile with a burning satisfaction and feeling of completeness.

This process is not necessarily easy. Your current subconscious program might not believe it at first. It might resist, making it hard for you to think about it. But you must resist this resistance, command your thoughts, and define your goal anyway. Think big. No limitations.

Do this:

1. Find a blank piece of paper and a pen.
2. Set an alarm on your phone for 20 minutes.

3. Now, write down ALL of your wildest dreams on that paper. NO LIMITATIONS!

4. When 20 minutes are up, stop.

5. Take a break for 30 minutes (take a walk).

6. After the break, look at the list and see what jumps up from the paper and into your heart.

7. Lastly, choose one of these dreams as your ultimate goal/biggest desire.

When your ultimate goal is set, do the following:

1. **Imagine in Detail**: First, imagine how it would feel to have accomplished your ultimate goal. Visualize in detail what you want to see. If you want to earn a certain amount of money, think about what you would buy with that money. Is it a villa? Picture the villa—how does it look? How does it smell? What furniture is there? If it's a car, what car is it? How does the car sound? How does it feel to drive it? How does the leather smell? Imagine everything in as many details as possible.

2. **Write Your Story**: Now, write down a story about having achieved your ultimate goal in the present tense. Include as many details as possible to spark your imagination. Engage as many of your five senses as possible: describe the feelings, smells, tastes, sights, and sounds. Write it in a way that gives you goosebumps. Make it real. Make it now.

3. **Take a Break**: Relax for 30 minutes. Take a walk, meditate, or do something calming.

4. **Refine Your Story**: Come back to your manuscript of your ultimate future and refine it. Write it cleanly so that when you read it, it brings up all the mental pictures you need to activate as many of your five senses as possible.

5. **Daily Affirmation**: Read this story out loud to yourself every day for the next 12 months.

Step 2: Commit Yourself

In life, you must commit to what you want to achieve. Dedicate your focus, time, and energy to your goals. One powerful way to do this is by writing a commitment letter to yourself. Frame this letter and hang it somewhere where you can see it often. A commitment letter should hit your emotions so hard that when you read it, you feel energized to keep going for another day. One of the strongest instincts in humans (if not the strongest) is the seeking of comfort. We seek what we are used to, looking for an easy way out. Life is not about ease and comfort, and it never will be for those wanting the life of their dreams. Easy is a habit. What seems hard now will become easier tomorrow, so commit yourself to reaching your ultimate goal. Commit yourself to go all in for the next 12 months. When you commit, you act with massive power. This is what you must do to succeed in achieving what you truly want in life. It is a marathon, not a sprint. It is a journey, not a destination. You must learn to love the process. You must learn to fall in love with your journey over and over again as you move toward your ultimate goal.

My commitment letter to myself is:

Here I stand, right now, with a burning passion in my soul and a heart beating fiercely for my future. With everything that I am, I vow to give all I can to achieve far more in my life. I will set goals so bold, so fearless, that they make me tremble—but I know they will ignite the fire within me and push me to face my challenges head-on.

My commitment is stronger than ever. Every single day, I will rise and work hard, move forward, and no matter how many times I fall, I will stand back up. For I know that it's not just possible for me to reach my goals—I must reach them.

People around me will see my resolve. My determination will shine so brightly that they will know I am invincible. Not because I am special, but because I refuse to give up. Never.

Deep down, I feel that I am meant for great things. This isn't just a belief; it's a certainty that resonates throughout my entire being. It's up to me, and only me, to turn my dreams into reality. I am ready to take full responsibility and do whatever it takes. Every day, one focused step at a time.

And yes, I also promise to stay relentlessly committed to my ultimate goal and utilize all the tools and resources at my disposal. They will serve as my guiding star, a daily reminder of the goals I set for myself. This is not just a declaration—it's a pact, an agreement with myself, my future, and my unwavering will to achieve greatness.

Do this:

1. Read my above letter 3-5 times.
2. Find a blank piece of paper and a pen.
3. Write your own commitment letter (you can use mine as inspiration).

4. Print it and hang it in a place you visit often.

5. Look at it every day for the next 12 months.

6. Know it from the first letter to the last, and repeat it mentally several times a day.

Step 3: Evaluate Your Last 12 Months

No Average mind has ever grown into an Above Average mind without evaluating their life, personality, actions, habits, feelings, thoughts, and beliefs. One of my teachers, Brendon Burchard (bestselling author of *High Performance Habits*), taught me the importance of adopting high-performance habits. One of the key habits is to evaluate myself weekly.

Another mentor, Darren Hardy (founder of *Success* magazine), emphasized the importance of looking back before planning ahead. Darren has had the privilege of interviewing hundreds of extremely successful people and then transitioned into a career as an author. My favorite book of his is *The Compound Effect*. To rise above Average, you must do what those Above Average do. You are what you do on a daily basis. You become what you think about all day long.

Evaluating yourself every year is not only crucial for your personal growth but also essential for reaching your ultimate goal in life. A well-known quote says: "The definition of insanity is doing the same thing over and over again, expecting different results." This you must read again. This is exactly why evaluating your last 12 months becomes key.

Do this:

1. Find a blank piece of paper and a pen.

2. Now write the following down on it with space for your answers.

a. The 10 best things that happened to me last year:

b. I am most proud of the following three achievements I made last year:

c. My absolute greatest experiences from last year are:

d. Three personal improvements I have made in the past year are:

e. If I could turn back time and do something differently, it would be:

f. The following had the biggest impact on me (books, people, attitudes, etc.):

g. The wisest decisions I made last year were:

h. The most helpful deeds I did last year were:

i. The biggest risks I took last year were:

j. The most important relationships I improved last year were:

k. Describe the entire last year in one word:

l. Three things I need to do less of in the coming new year are:

m. Three things I need to do more of in the coming new year are:

n. Three things I have to completely stop within the coming new year are:

3. Spend at least 3-5 hours answering these questions. You must be brutally honest.

4. Do this every year. The same questions provide new insights year after year.

Step 4: Identify Your Worst Habits

In my first book (available only in Danish), I focused on helping people change their habits. I was inspired to write it after coaching over 4,000 individuals to achieve better lifestyles and bodies they could enjoy, rather than fear or shame. Through this experience, I realized that humans do not change habits until their neuro associations change. Neuro associations are what your mind links with your actions. If it associates something positive, you will continue doing it. If it associates something negative, you will stop.

In Part III of this book, I shared a story about a woman whose daughter looked out the car window one morning while driving to school and wished her mother could run next to her while she was biking, just like one of her classmates' moms. This changed everything for the mother. This shifted her neuro associations regarding being overweight. She lost 20 kg in 4 months. Instead of associating weight loss with pain, such as the pain caused by having to change her diet, planning gym sessions, spending time traveling to the gym, losing "the good things" in life, giving up pizza four times a week, and feeling embarrassed at the gym, she began associating not losing weight with pain—like not living up to her child's needs, not being a good mother, not being a role model, and not doing what it takes to give her daughter what she needed. Instead of associating pleasure with eating candy several times a week, lounging on the couch binge-watching Netflix, and sticking to her usual routine, she started associating pleasure with becoming a role model for her daughter, living longer to see her grandchildren, feeling more attractive, and becoming proud of her accomplishments. This is the key to real change.

Do this:

1. Find a blank piece of paper and a pen.

2. Write "Bad Habits" at the top of the paper.

3. Set an alarm for 20 minutes.

4. Empty your mind of all habits that are not contributing to your long-term happiness.

5. When the alarm goes off, take a 30-minute break (go for a walk or do something relaxing).

6. Now take a new blank piece of paper and make space for three columns.

7. In column one, write "Habit," in column two, write "Pleasure," and in column three, write "Pain."

8. For each bad habit, think about what pains you get for NOT changing the habit.

9. For each bad habit, think about what pleasure you get when you DO change the habit.

10. Place this paper next to your bed and read it every morning before you start your day.

11. Do this until all bad habits are giving you the feeling of real pain when executing them.

12. Do not stop this process until the bad habits feel really bad for you.

Step 5: Define the Best Version of Yourself

Within every person on this planet lies an urge for true greatness. We are all born great. We are miracles of the universe, designed to strive for greatness and make the world a better place. We are born to make a difference, but we are programmed not to do so. Society teaches us to be fearful, anxious, disbelieving, negative, and angry. We are not born this way; we are programmed this way. Ask any 10-year-old if they wish to be angry, hateful, anxious, negative, or afraid. Not a single child would say yes. We are not born to be this way; we are taught to become this way.

You must learn to override your current programming with a new, better, and updated program. This is simple but not easy. It requires daily practice. This is not magic; it is pure training. Some of the greatest Hollywood actors do this as a profession. They practice their characters so intensely that they lose touch with their own selves.

Lady Gaga has publicly described the feeling of being out of touch with herself, feeling as if she were still on the set while taking a walk in the city. She experienced a "disconnect" from her own sense of self and the people in her personal life. Jim Carrey has described the painful process of rediscovering himself when he realized that Jim Carrey was depressed. Hollywood actors are trained in this process. They use psychotherapy and hypnotherapy to recreate their own selves and to develop new characters. So must you. To develop the character you want to be in your life, you must train yourself to become this character. To be someone, you must become someone.

Do this:

1. Find a blank piece of paper and a pen.

2. Write at the top: "The Best Version of Me."

3. Set a timer for 30 minutes.

4. Write as if you are already the best version of yourself, in the present tense.

5. Describe how you are, how you look, how it feels to be you, how you interact with others, your core values, the decisions you make, the actions you take, the habits and routines you maintain, your work, your earnings, and your ideal living situation. Include details about your physical health and appearance, how you manage stress, how you overcome challenges, and your overall emotional well-being. For example, "I am calm in the face of adversity and find joy in the little things every day." Write everything you can imagine.

6. Take a break for 30 minutes. Go for a walk or do something relaxing.

7. Return to your writing. Refine it, improve it, and transform it into a script that allows you to vividly see the mental pictures and feel the emotions of this new character. It should spark images that ignite emotions. You must feel it to believe it's real.

8. Read this script out loud twice every day. Feel what it's like to be this person.

9. Now, go out and be this person.

Step 6: Define Your Life 10 Years from Now

Average and Below Average minds do not have a clear vision of where they will be 10 years from now. This is something you must create. You need a vision for your future. Understand that your subconscious mind will guide your life based on the program it is running. Most people have never made any effort to reprogram their mind. With the Above Average Method, you will learn how to do this, bringing everything you dream of into your life. You must believe it before you see it. To believe is to have complete faith, without a single drop of doubt.

As you currently believe in wherever you are going now, you must change that to a destination designed by you through mental training. The believing part is difficult, but what you believe, you will receive. This is something you can practice and reprogram. Your destination must be clear, and your practice must be persistent. Most people get stuck on how to do it, whereas the real focus should be on WHERE and WHY. When you believe, the "how" will come to you just as you learned to walk. As a baby, you did not have the ability to disbelieve. You saw what others were doing and copied them until you started walking, talking, writing, and calculating.

Do this:

1. Find a blank piece of paper and a pen.

2. At the top of the page, write: "My Life Today."

3. Close your eyes for a moment and imagine yourself 10 years from now. Think about where you are, what you're doing, who you are with, and how you feel.

4. Set a timer for 30 minutes.

5. Begin writing as if you are living your life 10 years from now, using the present tense to make it vivid and real.

   a. Detail what a typical day looks like for you, including your routines, work, leisure activities, and interactions with others.

   b. Describe your achievements and personal growth. What skills have you mastered? What accomplishments are you most proud of?

c. Write about your relationships with family, friends, and significant others. How have they evolved? Are there new people in your life?

d. Where do you live? Describe your home and why it's ideal for you. How does it reflect your personal style and preferences?

e. Describe the habits you've adopted to maintain your physical and mental health. How do you balance stress and relaxation?

f. What are your passions and how do you pursue them? Have you taken up new hobbies or continued to develop existing ones?

6. As you describe your life, focus on how you feel about your achievements, relationships, and personal growth. Are you fulfilled, happy, and content? Why?

7. When the alarm goes off, say out loud to yourself: "I am now taking a quantum leap. I know exactly where I am going, and I am open to the unexpected."

8. Read this script every day and always end it with: "I am now taking a quantum leap. I know exactly where I am going, and I am open to the unexpected." Remember the date!

Step 7: Reprogram Your Mind for 60 Minutes Every Day

You have now been given some of the most effective tools to reprogram your mind and have read valuable information to embody these techniques in your daily life. Above Average minds are not born with this knowledge. They are born just like you, but their environment teaches them everything: their beliefs, habits, skills, attitudes, fears, and more. You are born for greatness, but your early environment programs you. You are a product of those who raised you and the friends you surrounded yourself with. Everything you see and feel around you is shaped by that.

The good news is that you are not destined to remain there. If you find yourself in the wrong story, start rewriting it! The question is: What IS your story? By now, you have designed new narratives. By now, you have taken steps to become bigger than your environment. This is the power humans possess. This is the power you will now bring to life. To do so, you must reprogram your mind every single day. You must immerse yourself in new patterns of thinking and behaving that align with the vision you have for your future. Reprogramming your mind requires consistent daily effort because the neural pathways of your old habits and beliefs are deeply ingrained. You must dedicate at least 20 minutes every day to reinforce your new narratives and empower yourself to overcome your previous limitations. This is the only way to reclaim your greatness. Remember, you are born a genius. The rest is purely programming.

Do this:

1. Spend at least 10 minutes every day reading the best version of yourself out loud to yourself.

2. Spend at least 10 minutes every day reading your life 10 years from now out loud to yourself.

3. Spend at least 10 minutes every day reading your bad habits out loud to yourself.

4. Spend at least 10 minutes every day reading your commitment letter out loud to yourself.

5. Spend at least 20 minutes every day to mentally see, feel, and reread these things throughout your day.

Step 8: Introduce Deep Work

I was first introduced to this concept in Cal Newport's bestselling book, *Deep Work*. Deep Work involves dedicating your full attention to one task at a time, shutting out all distractions—no phone, no breaks, just 100% focus. To achieve your goals, you must learn to work in 'Deep Work' mode. It takes an average of 20-30 minutes to enter a Flow State. In this state, whatever you are working on flows effortlessly from your mind to the paper or computer screen. Time stands still, and your creativity and focus are at their peak. A single notification or browser diversion can break this flow, requiring you to spend the same amount of time to regain it. You can compare this to Conor McGregor (UFC champion and very wealthy entrepreneur) being distracted by an audience member while in a fight. It's clear that such a distraction would lead to his defeat. Similarly, you must enter "The Zone" of focus when working on your goals. This will save you time, allowing you to spend it on what truly matters: your family and friends. Moreover, it will enable you to produce quality work.

Do this:

1. Plan your week ahead every week.

2. When planning your week, include only two things in your calendar: Appointments and Time Blocks.

   - Appointments: These are meetings, lunches, or other plans that require you to be somewhere at a specific time.

- Time Blocks: These are periods you set aside for tasks and projects. This is where Deep Work comes into play.

3. Review your list of goals for the next 12 months.

4. Schedule as many tasks as possible into your calendar. These will be Time Blocks for Deep Work.

5. Start by spending at least one hour of Deep Work on each task during the first week.

6. Increase your Deep Work time by 15 minutes each week until you can stay completely focused for 2-3 hours on a task. If a task is finished before the allocated time, take a 15-minute break and move on to the next one.

7. Stay 100% true to your calendar. Your calendar is your success recipe, and you must follow it meticulously.

Do this for the rest of the year, and you will reach your goals faster.

Step 9: Reject Negative Thoughts All Day

Negative thoughts will always try to intrude. You can't eliminate them, but you can learn to reject them. You have the power to control your thoughts. Let's try an exercise. Think about a blue elephant. Visualize it. A blue elephant. Do you see it? Good. Now switch to a black cat. Do you see it? That's proof. You have complete control over your thoughts and mental images.

You can choose to think and visualize whatever you want in your mind. If you find yourself thinking more negatively than positively, it's just a matter of practice and time. Your neural pathways will adapt to what you do most frequently. The more you reject negative thoughts and replace them with positive ones, the stronger those positive neural pathways will become, eventually becoming automatic. While most people see problems, the Above Average mind sees opportunities. Where the majority sees worst-case scenarios, the Above Average mind envisions the best possible outcomes. Where most people fear change, the Above Average mind embraces it.

This is a program—a neural pathway program. Neurons that fire together, wire together.

Do this:

1. Become aware of your thoughts.

2. When you become aware of negative thoughts, decide to reject them.

3. When you reject a negative thought, immediately replace it with a positive one.

4. For effective replacement, find the exact opposite of your negative thought. For instance:

   - If you often think, "I can't do it," replace it with, "I can do it."

   - If you often think, "I am always so unlucky," replace it with, "I am always lucky."

   - If you often think, "I can never make this amount of money," replace it with, "I am making this amount of money."

5. Do this for the rest of your life.

Step 10: Establish An Exercise Routine

You must understand that your body is the home of your soul, and your soul uses your body to manifest everything it wants. Your body is the place you will always live in, so treat it well.

Obesity, anxiety, lifestyle diseases, and depression have been rising in recent decades. It doesn't take a genius to figure this out: you are what you eat. You must understand that the capitalist world does not care about your health. They care about themselves and their earnings. The capitalist wants to earn as much money as possible. Michael Easter wrote a book called *The Comfort Crisis*, highlighting how terribly comfortable the majority of people have become and what the consequences are and will be. You are not born to overeat. You are not born to spend 10 hours in front of the TV. You are not born to spend four hours scrolling through social media. The majority of people have fallen into this trap. Many experts have pointed this out.

World statistics show this fact: we are becoming more overweight and mentally sick than ever before. You must understand that working out or moving more than you ever have is healthy for you. The more energy your body has, the longer you live and the more you can do without feeling drained, stressed, and depressed. Your body is your temple.

Take good care of it starting today and for the rest of your life.

Do this:

1. If you are new to strength training: Invest in a personal trainer for a minimum of six months.

2. If you are used to strength training but do not train: Invest in a personal trainer for a minimum of six months.

3. If you are used to strength training and train once in a while: Plan to go to the gym at least four times a week.

4. If you are a single parent and do not find time to train: Make it a priority and find the time.

5. If you are above 45 years old and have not been training for years: Invest in a personal trainer for a minimum of six months.

6. Do not plan to work out less than four times a week.

7. Get it done!

Now that you have the first 10 steps down, let's finish the rest to get to your Above Average mind!

CHAPTER 12

THE ABOVE AVERAGE METHOD - STEPS 11 TO 20

In the last chapter, we dove into the first ten steps to the Above Average Method. There are ten more to go!

Step 11: Evaluate Your Inner Circle

You are the average of the five people you spend the most time with. The people you surround yourself with will reinforce your subconscious programming. You are constantly influenced by the world around you, so you must be mindful of your surroundings. This includes the books you read, the podcasts you listen to, the news you follow, the parties you attend, the people who guide you, and, of course, your friends and family. Reflect on who truly brings value to your life and who does not. Spend more time with those who give you energy and less with those who drain your energy. This will make a significant difference in your life. Even your family might need a shift in terms of time spent, ideas shared, or advice taken. Choose wisely.

I am not saying you do not need good friends or love. All humans need these things. However, you must understand the difference between achieving your goals and love. Balance is essential, and cutting off good people is not the goal. Learn to recognize who is valuable in your life. Your ultimate goal is important, but so is maintaining balance. You need good people and diversity in your life, but you do not need energy drainers, negative people, hate, jealousy, or fear.

Do this:

1. Find a blank piece of paper and a pen.

2. Create a table on the paper. On the left side, list names, and on the right side, create three checkboxes labeled "Positive," "Negative," and "Neutral" next to each name.

3. List the people you spend the most time with. Include those you talk to and meet most often, those with whom you discuss your life, and those who advise you frequently.

4. Evaluate each person against your best self and ultimate life goal. Determine whether each person has a positive, negative, or neutral impact on your journey toward becoming your best self and achieving your ultimate goal.

5. Adjust your time accordingly. Spend more time with those who have a positive impact, less to no time with those who have a negative impact, and limit your attention to those who have a neutral impact.

Step 12: Take Massive Action

Understand that attracting good things in life does not happen without massive action. The concept of manifestation is widely misunderstood. Nothing will manifest itself without any action taken—nothing. You must stop believing that your goals will magically appear on your doorstep. They won't. We live in a physical world, but our minds possess a nonphysical realm where everything starts. You must believe it before you see it, but you will never see it in the physical world without taking action. Manifesting winning the lottery is pure madness, but you can manifest the person you want to become, the goals you want to achieve, and the life you want to live by taking massive action toward them.

Achieving your goals requires a combination of belief, faith, and action. As James 2:17 states, "In the same way, faith by itself, if it is not accompanied by action, is dead."

Do this:

1. Take a clean sheet of paper and write down today's date and your current goals.

2. List 10 goals you want to accomplish in the next 12 months. Ensure these align with your ultimate life goal and write them in the present tense. For example: "I earn," "I achieve," "I weigh," "I drive such and such a car," "I own," etc.

3. Identify the most impactful goal. Look at your list of ten goals and ask yourself: If I had a magic wand and could achieve any one goal within 24 hours, which goal would have the greatest positive impact on my life? Usually, one goal will stand out.

4. Circle that goal. Transfer it to a clean sheet of paper.

5. Write the one goal at the top of the paper in the present tense.

6. Set a deadline for achieving this goal.

7. Make a list of everything you need to do to accomplish it.

8. Organize this list into a checklist.

9. Take massive action. Do something every day that moves you closer to your goal until you achieve it.

Step 13: Create Your Daily Focus Plan

The majority of people spend too much time on activities that provide instant gratification but no real progress. Many spend around 2 hours a day on social media, and the average American adult watches three to four hours of TV per day. Consider this: on average, we have about 4,000 weeks from birth until we leave this planet. If you spend six hours a day on social media or watching TV, out of 16 waking hours, it amounts to 19.6 weeks a year, which is 38% of a whole year.

The Above Average mind knows that time is the one thing that can never be recovered, and focus is the tool to master time. Time is an illusion; there is only life and death, memories, and future visions. Your subconscious mind does not understand time, while your conscious mind perceives it as memories and future vision. Think about it: does what happened five minutes ago still exist? Does what you plan to do tomorrow exist? No, there is only now, and you must learn to understand this. Be present in the moment and make the most of your life.

As my mentor Brendon Burchard once said, "When I lie in my bed in my last hours of life, I will reflect on three questions: Did I live? Did I love? Did I matter?" You must learn to be focused and present with the ones you love. This can only be achieved fully if you have a plan.

Do this:

1. Take a clean sheet of paper and write down your goal for this year in today's state.

2. Create space for five lines under the headline: "Five big things I must do to move this project forward."

3. In the middle of the paper, write in big letters: "PEOPLE."

4. To the left below "PEOPLE," write: "People I need to reach out to today." List the people you must contact today, no matter what, and create five lines for their names.

5. To the right below "PEOPLE," write: "People I'm waiting on." List the people from whom you need something to move forward, and create five lines for their names.

6. Below, in the middle, write in big letters: "PRIORITIES."

7. Under "PRIORITIES," write: "The main things I must complete today, no matter what." List the priorities and tasks that must be accomplished today. Do these before getting trapped in your inbox and other people's agendas, and create five lines for these tasks.

8. Fill this out every morning before you start your day.

9. Focus solely on your five priorities for that day.

10. Repeat this process daily for the rest of your life.

Step 14: Establish an Above Average Morning Routine

Successful people are simply individuals with successful routines. The Above Average minds understand this. You must establish a morning routine that consists of essential activities. These should include meditation, visualization, autosuggestion, physical exercise, reading, and planning your day. I've encountered thousands of people who aspire to be the best in their industry but never read about it. I've met hundreds of salespeople who want to maximize their earnings but never read a sales book. I've met countless leaders who desire a well-functioning, effective, and happy team but never read about leadership, human motivation, or psychology. To rise Above Average, you must do what the Average person does not.

Do this:

1. Plan to have two to three hours for yourself in the morning.

2. If this is challenging, go to bed two or three hours earlier.

3. Follow this routine as a starting point and adjust it to your needs:

    a. Wake up two to three hours before work.

    b. Start your day with 5-20 minutes of meditation.

    c. Visualize the best version of yourself achieving your ultimate goal for 10-15 minutes. Feel as though it has already happened and believe it is already done with complete faith.

    d. Take a walk for 20-30 minutes while practicing autosuggestion. Suggest to yourself how amazing today will be and express gratitude for your achievements. Do this aloud while you walk. If you find this embarrassing initially, do it mentally.

    e. Spend 15-30 minutes reading a book that guides you toward a better version of yourself or your ultimate goal in life. It could be a book like this one.

f. Spend the last 10-15 minutes on your daily focus plan.

g. Do this every day for the rest of your life.

Step 15: Establish an Above Average Evening Routine

As discussed earlier, the majority of people spend three to four hours watching TV every day. Cristiano Ronaldo does not. If he watches TV, it's to study his opponents and prepare himself. Think like Cristiano Ronaldo! You will be surprised how much time you gain by removing TV from your life. This is part of the comfort crisis. Do not fall for this trap. Instead, establish an evening routine that winds your mind down and inspires it for tomorrow. In the evening, right before you fall asleep, you have a golden opportunity to reprogram your mind. There is a small time gap to suggest inspiring self-confidence and clear directions to your subconscious mind.

Do this:

1. Train yourself to go to bed no later than 10 p.m.

2. When in bed, after spending time with your partner, select a sentence to mentally command your subconscious mind to believe in.

3. If you're worried about waking up on time, suggest to your subconscious mind the exact time you want to wake up before you sleep, and it will wake you up.

4. Command your subconscious mind to start thinking, feeling, being, and acting as the best version of yourself.

5. Affirm to your subconscious mind that you are whole, perfect, strong, powerful, loving, harmonious, and happy.

6. Affirm that you are living your ultimate goal in life now.

7. Express gratitude, close your eyes, and go to sleep.

8. Repeat this routine every night for the rest of your life.

Step 16: Establish an Above Average Weekly Routine

Humans learn from experience, but only if experience forces them to change. We learn from pain, failures, mistakes, and tough times. However, most people wait too long to learn because they don't see their mistakes until they cause pain. We are biologically programmed to seek pleasure and avoid pain, which is why bad habits form and why we avoid stepping out of our comfort zones. You must understand that any drama in your life is mental drama. Learn to assess yourself and your actions before they become painful. Once pain occurs, the damage is already done. You can control and avoid this.

Do this:

1. Spend 60 minutes every week with a pen and paper answering these six questions. Be honest in your responses. Awareness of your actions is crucial. Avoid the ego trap of self-denial. Real change starts with the truth:

   - What did I do this week?
   - What did I learn this week?
   - What must I become better at next week?
   - What must I do differently next week and how?
   - What are my top five priorities next week?
   - What was I grateful for this week?

2. Repeat this process every week for the rest of your life.

Step 17: Remove Yourself from Screens

By now, you must understand how social media, emails, and other distractions constantly pull your attention away. One of humanity's greatest mental challenges is maintaining focus. Our attention span has decreased from 12 seconds to approximately 8 seconds—less than a goldfish's 9 seconds. You must realize that Big Tech companies profit from our engagement; their product is you, me, all of us. The more we use their platforms, the richer they get, exploiting our dopamine, the chemical that makes us feel good. This addiction is fundamentally changing how we think. Many people feel more stressed, anxious, and depressed as a result of constantly reacting to stimuli instead of being proactive.

Throughout your day, you're engaged in two types of conversations: with others and with yourself. Whenever you open your phone, computer, TV, or radio, your brain starts a conversation with itself, reacting to what you see and hear. You don't always control the thoughts that arise—you are reacting. In our tech-driven era, we are constantly talking to ourselves because of technology, reacting instead of controlling our thoughts or experiencing complete silence. When was the last time you experienced complete silence?

Social media exposes you and your children (or future children) to a wide range of emotions. We are not built to handle such intense emotional diversity at the rate we do today. Seeing something that makes you envious or sad triggers a cascade of thoughts and emotions. Your brain can't distinguish between fantasy and reality, so it all feels real. To manage this, you must remove yourself from screens in your daily life.

Do this:

1. Cut down your screen time by 30 minutes a day starting now.

2. Next week, reduce your screen time by an additional 15 minutes.

3. The week after, cut it down by another 15 minutes.

4. Continue reducing by 15 minutes each week.

5. Keep reducing until you are proactively seeking information from screens rather than reacting to urges. If you react to the urge, you've lost to Big Tech again.

6. Delete all apps from your phone that you haven't used in the last four weeks. You don't need them.

7. Spend time on social media for business purposes only.

8. Unfollow any account that triggers negative emotions in you.

9. Follow social media accounts that make you smarter, emotionally fit, and happy. These could be self-development or role model accounts.

10. Start this process now.

Step 18: Invest in a Mentor or a Mentor Program

I had never invested in mentors until I made my biggest and best investment in two, and they eventually became investors in my business. I didn't cash out; I gave them 75% of my company. One of them is the Godfather of the food delivery industry and the founder of JustEat.com. The other is the Godfather of nightclubs in Scandinavia and an investor in several large corporations. They invested $150,000 in my idea, and I went for it. Fifteen years later, that company is the largest fashion marketplace in Europe, generating over $300 million in yearly turnover. You can certainly achieve a lot on your own, but to become Above Average, you must do what Above Average people do: invest in mentors or mentorship programs.

This doesn't mean finding someone who will give you all the answers. It means connecting with someone who has walked the path before you, someone who can guide you through challenges with wisdom and insight. Above Average minds all invest in mentors or mentor programs. Personally, I invest 3% of my yearly income in mentors. Over the past decade, I've invested over $500,000. This investment has enabled me to build businesses faster, earn more than the majority in a short time, coach others to do the same, and much more. A mentor brings more to the table than just advice. A mentor provides perspective, accountability, and a network of contacts that can open doors you didn't even know existed. A mentor moves you from unconscious incompetence to conscious competence faster than anything else. There are thousands of things you don't know. Without mentors, I wouldn't be where I am today. Without mentors, you will not reach your ultimate goal or full potential.

Do this:

1. Take a close look at your ultimate goal and think about what qualities, skills, experiences, and knowledge you need to achieve it.

2. Write these down on a blank piece of paper.

3. Identify the top five most important items on the list.

4. Write these top five items on the backside of the paper.

5. Spend at least 20 hours this year searching for mentors or mentorship programs that can teach you these essential things.

6. Invest a minimum of 3% of your yearly income in a mentor or a mentorship program.

7. Repeat this process every year until you reach your ultimate goal.

Step 19: Establish Your MasterMind Group

You must spend the majority of your time working on your goal list. Dedicate at least two to four hours each month speaking with people who are or have been in the same industry, have accomplished similar goals, or have experience in crucial areas you need to master to reach your ultimate goal. When I started my first company, one of my mentors had succeeded in another industry with a similar business model. My other mentor had scaled and exited major companies and was highly respected in the Scandinavian business community.

As we built the company, I spoke with several industry leaders on a monthly basis. Today, I speak with some of the best in my industry on Zoom calls once or twice each month. The knowledge, support, and joint venture opportunities this has given me are invaluable and couldn't be bought for any amount of money. You must create a small network of experts that you meet or speak with monthly. Be brave enough to reach out to them, knowing what you want to accomplish, sharing your visions, and being transparent about your intention to start a MasterMind group. Know what you can bring to the table, and make them value you for who you are, what you know, and what you can do for them. Good energy always wins.

Do this:

1. Define the purpose of creating your MasterMind group. What do you want to accomplish with it? Personal development? Career goals? Your ultimate goal?

2. Look for five to seven people who are among the best in the industry. Reach out to them with a professional email. Attend events where they might be and speak to them. Leverage your network to find mutual connections. Make a concerted effort!

3. Agree on the first MasterMind meeting date.

4. Establish your MasterMind rules and an agenda.

5. In the first meeting, discuss what each member wants to achieve with the group. Ensure everyone gains something valuable in return for their time spent together.

6. Evaluate your MasterMind group every quarter. Identify who is participating with quality, who is not, who contributes positively, and who does not.

7. Discuss improvements to the group and keep going.

8. Hold at least one MasterMind meeting every month, either digitally or physically. Digital meetings are preferable for efficiency.

Step 20: Establish an Above Average Yearly Routine

Most people celebrate the new year without reflecting on what they learned from the previous year. While everyone has the desire to improve, few take the time to review their accomplishments, lessons learned, necessary changes, relationships to cut or build, subjects to study, ways to work better, and plans to become better and more loving and giving. Most people set

New Year's resolutions only to fail by April. The Above Average mind becomes better year after year by reflecting, evaluating, planning, setting priorities, executing, tweaking, adjusting, and repeating. If you want to achieve your ultimate goal in life, you must do the same.

Remember, this book is for those who want to rise to Above Average. If you truly want it, you can do it. By studying this book daily for the next twelve months and implementing the Above Average Method, you will succeed. You must also teach this book to others. Teaching occurs when you know the material well. You must know to become Above Average.

Do this:

1. At the end of each year, block out at least five hours daily for a minimum of five days.

2. Review and repeat Steps 1 to 20.

3. Commit to doing this for the rest of your life!

CONCLUSION:
ONE LIFE TO LIVE

Life is precious, my friend. Why? Because you only live once. You have one life, one opportunity, and before you know it, it's gone. It passes quickly, and then it's game over. Humans are meant to create, express ourselves, expand, and explore, yet many choose not to, held back by fear-filled narratives. Remember, fear is an illusion, while mistakes are real. We must fail before we can succeed. We must learn before we can improve. We must act before we can perfect.

Every person's journey toward their dreams starts with a decision—not just any decision, but one that propels them away from mediocrity and toward the life they truly desire. In this book, I've tried to capture the essence of living Above Average, to inspire you to reach for the life you want. Understanding these principles is the first step, but it's not enough. You must implement these strategies into your own life and continuously act on your dreams. This is what truly separates those who dream from those who achieve.

You now have the tools, the knowledge, and the strategies. It's up to you to put them into practice. Each day is a new canvas, an opportunity to move closer to the life you've envisioned. As you've learned, to truly rise Above Average, you must surround yourself with like-minded achievers who support and push you toward your goals. The company you keep profoundly influences your mindset. To see this, put this book away and return to your normal life for 21 days. When you come back, you'll find yourself starting over. Your environment shapes you. To rise Above Average, you must (1) Study this book's information, (2) Implement the Above Average Methods weekly, and (3) Teach the Method to those seeking a successful and fulfilling life. Only then will the book's insights manifest. Growth comes to those who seek it. Do you want to grow?

Remember, life isn't just about the goals we achieve but the journey, growth, and transformation along the way. The joy lies in the steps toward our goals. You are born to grow and expand your consciousness. Celebrate your progress in applying the Above Average Method, not just the outcomes. Every small victory, every resilient moment, and every courageous decision to choose growth over comfort is a testament to your commitment to rising Above Average.

As you near the end of this book, you might feel a mix of excitement and apprehension. That's natural. It means you're on the edge of your comfort zone, ready for significant changes. I salute and cheer you on! These feelings signal your readiness to transition into a new life phase, where your decisions align with your dreams.

Remember, change comes with challenges and setbacks. Embrace them. Each challenge is a lesson; every setback sets up a comeback. I'm not a motivational speaker, but I am a realist.

This is the reality successful people understand and accept. Your ability to persevere, learn, and adapt will define your journey.

As your life changes, so too might your definitions of success and fulfillment. Be flexible and ready to adapt the Above Average Method to your evolving needs and circumstances. The Method remains constant while your perspectives and growth evolve. Implementing this method yearly, I've seen continuous growth for over a decade. Life is good!

As this book closes, your real work begins. Shift from learning to doing, from consuming to creating, from following to leading. Set clear, actionable goals for the next week, month, and year. Break them into steps you can start immediately. Momentum is key, and building it starts small, scaling efforts as you gain confidence and see results. Success leaves traces. Study those who have succeeded, implement their ways, and you'll achieve similar results.

The million-dollar question: Are you willing to do it?

Above all, stay committed to your growth. Revisit this book's principles, reflect on your experiences, and continuously refine your approach. Teach others through your actions, becoming a living example of an Above Average life. As we conclude, ask yourself, on a scale of 1 to 10, how much do you want to grow? How far will you push your potential? Your decision will determine your life's trajectory. Choose wisely, act boldly, and never settle for Average.

This is your time to shine, to rise Above Average, and to make your life a masterpiece. Let's begin.

A NOTE FROM THE AUTHOR: LAST WORDS BEFORE YOU TAKE ACTION

C ongratulations on finishing this entire book. This is an accomplishment in itself. Celebrate it! Studies show that more than half of adults haven't read a book in a full year. Over 20% haven't read a book in more than three years, and more than 25% of those who start a book never finish it. You are among the few who saw it through. This already puts you on the path to an Above Average mind. It shows how badly you want it. This is just the beginning. Your journey truly starts now.

From now on, take the massive actions we've discussed throughout this book. All these words, ideas, and strategies mean nothing if they remain in your head. It is time to take action! You have armed yourself with knowledge; now you must step it up and do the work. Remember, every big achiever and every success story began with someone deciding to do something different—to not just dream but to do. This is what you must do as well. This is your destiny.

I suggest reading the book again while you are completing the Above Average Method. Read, reread, teach, and study the book over and over again. Each time you read it, I promise you will experience new levels of awareness. The Above Average Method will serve you better this way. This is a fact.

Your thoughts and beliefs must evolve for you to transform. You must embody the person you aspire to be. Follow the guidance in this book and do so with immense dedication. This is your path to success. Understand that the challenge is primarily mental. It is an illusion because, in reality, the hardest thing would be to stay stagnant and not pursue your true potential.

So, close this book not just feeling inspired but ready to accelerate into action. You're prepared. You have everything you need. Now, let's see what you can achieve. This is not the end; it's the beginning of your extraordinary journey. Live the rest of your life Above Average and thrive.

SOURCES

- *Unlimited Power* by Tony Robbins
- *Becoming Supernatural* by Dr. Joe Dispenza
- *Breaking the Habit of Being Yourself* by Dr. Joe Dispenza
- *You Are the Placebo* by Dr. Joe Dispenza
- *Mind to Matter* by Dawson Church
- *The Power of Your Subconscious Mind* by Joseph Murphy
- *Think and Grow Rich* by Napoleon Hill
- *The Comfort Crisis* by Michael Easter
- *Here's Help!* by M.R. Kopmeyer
- *How to Get Whatever You Want* by M.R. Kopmeyer
- *The Big Book of NLP, Expanded: 350+ Techniques, Patterns & Strategies of Neuro Linguistic Programming* by Shlomo Vaknin
- *The NLP Practitioner Manual* by Peter Freeth
- *Get the Life You Want: The Secrets to Quick and Lasting Life Change with Neuro-Linguistic Programming* by Richard Bandler

- *Instant Self-Hypnosis: How to Hypnotize Yourself with Your Eyes Open* by Forbes Robbins Blair
- *Neuro-linguistic Programming for Dummies* by Kate Burton & Romilla Ready
- *Time Line Therapy and the Basis of Personality* by Tad James & Wyatt Woodsmall
- *The Science of Getting Rich* by Wallace D. Wattles
- *You 2: A High Velocity Formula for Multiplying Your Personal Effectiveness in Quantum Leaps* by PricePritchett
- *Mastering the Rockefeller Habits* by Verne Harnish
- *10x Is Easier Than 2x: How World-Class Entrepreneurs Achieve More by Doing Less* by Dan Sullivan & Dr. Benjamin Hardy
- *The 48 Laws of Power* by Robert Greene
- *The Laws of Human Nature* by Robert Greene
- *12 Rules for Life: An Antidote to Chaos* by Jordan B. Peterson
- *High Performance Habits: How Extraordinary People Become That Way* by Brendon Burchard
- *No Excuses!: The Power of Self-Discipline* by Brian Tracy
- *Finish What You Start: The Art of Following Through, Taking Action, Executing, & Self-Discipline* byPeter Hollins
- *Excuses Begone!: How to Change Lifelong, Self-Defeating Thinking Habits* by Dr. Wayne Dyer
- *The Daily Stoic* by Ryan Holiday
- *Who Dares Wins: Special Forces Heroes of the SAS* by Pete Scholey
- *You Were Born Rich* by Bob Proctor

- *Change Your Paradigm, Change Your Life* by Bob Proctor
- *The Art of Living* by Bob Proctor
- *Thoughts Are Things: Turning Your Ideas Into Realities* by Bob Proctor & Greg S. Reid
- *The Strangest Secret* by Earl Nightingale
- *The Power of Awareness* by Neville Goddard
- *The Power of Now: A Guide to Spiritual Enlightenment* by Eckhart Tolle
- *Areté: Activate Your Heroic Potential* by Brian Johnson
- *Mindsight: The New Science of Personal Transformation* by Daniel J. Siegel
- *Principles* by Ray Dalio
- *Rich Dad Poor Dad* by Robert Kiyosaki
- *Millionaire Success Habits* by Dean Graziosi
- *Ego Is the Enemy* by Ryan Holiday
- *Man's Search for Meaning* by Viktor Frankl
- *The Science of Subtle Energy: The Healing Power of Dark Matter* by Yury Kronn, Jurriaan Kamp & BruceLipton
- *You Create Your Life—quantum physics explains how* by Henning R. Jensen
- *The 5 AM Club* by Robin Sharma
- *The Monk Who Sold His Ferrari* by Robin Sharma
- **The Creative Process in the Individual by <u>Thomas Troward</u>**
- **Change yout thoughts, change your life by Wayne Dyer**

Web Brainwaves:

https://www.linkedin.com/pulse/how-brainwaves-can-help-child-parent-rohan-girdhani/

Everything is energy: https://www.youtube.com/watch?v=GCt1luhLmZg

Healing yourself (subconscious mind): https://www.youtube.com/watch?v=ClCJjKeFmbk

Dr.Joe Dispenza:https://www.youtube.com/watch?v=rOYlOdDgYUU&t=66s

Dr.Joe Dispenza:https://www.youtube.com/watch?v=d7sUWwHugg8

ACKNOWLEDGMENTS

I want to acknowledge my team, Caspar Kjær, Sebastian S. Dyrgaard and Andreas Tankmar who's been with me in my ups and downs. I want to Acknowledge my Dad, John Radoor who's always there to listen, support og teach me how to be a better man. I also want to Acknowledge Hasmark Publishing for believing in me and my manuscript; for without all of you and your help, this book would not be possible. From my heart I thank you and wish for you all the best in life.

ABOUT THE AUTHOR

Mike Radoor is living proof that rising above average is a choice anyone can make, no matter where they start.

Growing up in the tough, working-class neighborhood of Odense, Denmark, Mike was no stranger to hardship. His father's battle with mental illness cast a shadow over much of his childhood, and the community around him wasn't one that valued ambition or success. Most kids in his neighborhood weren't focused on excelling in school. Instead, shortcuts, minor criminal activities, and a lack of aspiration were common.

At just 9 years old, Mike's life took a drastic turn. A rollerblading accident where he ran in front of a car left him in a light coma, with brain damage and severe leg injuries. It was a life-altering moment—one that could have defined him in a negative way.

An average Danish Child, Mike was interested in soccer but after his traffic accident he was told that he would never play soccer again and most likely experience difficulties in school due to his brain injury. This message had a huge impact in Mike's attitude and for some reason he chose to challenge this. He brought with him to school a football everyday, he studied harder than ever before, but due to his brain injury Mike had challenges focusing in school which drove him to be a bit too energetic in school, resulting in loads of issues with his teachers. Mike did finish his assignments, he did do his homework, he did everything he could for not to be "different" than the other kids. Due to his energy and wants to be like everyone else, he quicky experienced heavy bullying in school. When Mike's mom and dad seperated they moved to another part of the city, resulting in change of school and new location to live. In this period Mike's mother was fighting for the familyes safety and financial situation which resulted in Mike and his bigger sister was forced to live seperated from their mom. Mike moved to his grandmother, his sister to some friends of his mother and his mother moved into her new boyfriend. This was a though period in Mike's upbringing which resultet in even more server bullying in Mike's new school where Mike did not have the same financial support as the other kids. Mike had to wear clothing which some of Mike's mothers friends donated, not always looking as new and trending as the other kids.

This created a huge drive in Mike for being accepted by the others. He finally started playing soccer again and with his determined mind, Mike quickly became one of the best soccerplayers in his age in the youth leauge he was playing. This resultet in Mike becoming popular and he got the taste for more. He quickly understood that effort equalices popularity which drove Mike to be more intense in his efforts.

Finishing groundschool Mike was getting some of the lowest grades, but in his last year he decided to change this, so he went intense into doing his homeworks and step it up. He was later on accepted on HHX (which is a business High School) and from here his growth was fast. He entered a national competition called Young Enterprise where more than 1.000 groups nationwide compeeted on creating an idea that would evolve into a real company. Mike and his team lost the first place, but became number 2 nationwide with the idea that 4 years later founded the foundation of miinto.com together with his childhood friend Konrad A. Kierklo.

After highschool Mike applied for a trainee position in KMPG as an auditor and got accepted, but 6 months later Mike didn't feel it was the right path in his career, so he quit and decided to move to Copenhagen to enter Copenhagen Business School. Mike was accepted and side by side Mike took a job as a bartender in the age of 20 years old in one of the capitals most famlous nightclubs. After 5 months as a weekend bartender, Mike was promoted to manage the Nightclub and within 9 months Mike took the Nightclub to record breaking revenue results. In the meantime Konrad had contacted Mike to suggest that they took the idea from High School and build a real company based on it. Both Mike and Konrad took a loan in the bank and while Konrad was working in KPMG and Mike was running the nightclub, they pursued the dream of creating one of the worlds largest online fashion marketplaces.

Due to Mike's results in the nightclub in such a quick pace and young age, Mike was invited to Miami by the nighclub King Carsten Mikkelsen. Carsten had just exited Justeat.com with a large multimillion cashout and in Miami, Carsten wanted Mike to run a global nightclub concept which Mike rejected hence his company with Konrad. Carsten decided to hear more about it and in 2009 Carsten Mikkelsen and Just Eat founder, Jesper Buch decided to invest $100.000 in Mike and Konrads business.

Mike decided to go all in together with Konrad and he dedicated his life to build his dream. Mike studied selfimprovement daily, he read and reread Unlimited Power by Tony Robbins, he studied Think and Grow rich and never lost sight of daily reading and implementations of the new knowledge he aqquired. In 2011 Mike was asked to move to Stockholm, Sweden to expand miinto.com. In 2012 miinto got it's first venture capital investment and Mike was asked to do exactly what he did in Sweden, now just in 6 other countries such as America, England, Spain, Ireland, Netherlands and Norway.

This period was though to Mike's mental health since he travled 2-3 times a week and lived on hotels in new countries almost every month. The loneliness and high growth pressure from their investors drove Mike into a breakdown with stress and anxiety. In 2015 Mike requested to be moved to Sweden to help turnaround the business and within 12 months that was the case. Mike had cleaned up the company and created a breakeven point which made the board aware of a better approach which meant that operations got shut down in Sweden and centralized and managed from the Danish headquarter. Due to Mike's mental health, he decided to resign from miinto, which was a devasting decision for Mike. He left his baby, but his mental health was more important and within 3 years Mike had founded 2 new companies. One in New York, Playbookapp.io and one in Stockholm, Ocast.com.

About 4 years later Mike had excited both miinto and playbookapp and decided to take a year off from building businesses, but it didn't take him long to find his true passion: coaching. He started a lifestyle coaching firm which did incredible well the first 2 years. From o to 900 clients a month, Mike had found his true call in life which enabled him to write his first book (Begynd Med Vanerne), Begin With The Habits.

In 2022 Mike decided to shut down his lifestyle coaching business to pursue his ultimate goal in life which is to inspire millions of people to create their highest life. In 2024 Mike had build a striving online coaching business which enabled people to dream big, structure up and break free from limiting beliefs to create the life of their dreams. After coaching +1.000 career focused people, Mike got a hinch from his intuition: It was time to enter the global market, which inspired him to write this book Above Average – The Science of Achievement.

Mike now travels the world to lecture people on how to become the absolute best version of themselves and create their highest life.

Anything is possible. Mike Radoor is proof.

Get Above Average Method Workbook FOR FREE

Visit www.aboveaveragemethod.com/workbook now